Adam to Ahab

Myth and History in the Bible

Frederick H. Stitt

Adam to Ahab

2005

Myth and History in the Bible

[FHS05]

Paragon House
St. Paul

138pp

First Edition 2005

Published in the United States by
Paragon House
1925 Oakcrest Avenue
St. Paul, MN 55113

Copyright © 2005 by Paragon House

Cover art: "Jonah" by Lika Tov, Jerusalem. Printed with permission.

> All rights reserved. No part of this book may be reproduced, in any form, without written permission from the publisher, unless by a reviewer who wishes to quote brief passages.

Library of Congress Cataloging-in-Publication Data

Stitt, Frederick H., 1929-
  Adam to Ahab : myth and history in the Bible / Frederick H. Stitt.-- 1st ed.
    p. cm.
  ISBN 1-55778-852-9 (pbk. : alk. paper) 1. Bible. O.T.--History of
Biblical events. 2. Myth in the Bible. 3. Bible. O.T.--Criticism,
interpretation, etc. I. Title.
  BS635.3.S75 2005
  221.6--dc22
                                2005003600

The paper used in this publication meets the minimum requirements of American National Standard for Information Sciences—Permanence of Paper for Printed Library Materials, ANSIZ39.48-1984.

Manufactured in the United States of America
10 9 8 7 6 5 4 3 2 1

For current information about all releases from Paragon House,
visit the web site at http://www.paragonhouse.com

Dedication

This book is dedicated to my wife, Suzanne, our eight children, and our ten grandchildren. Also, to the University of Chicago, and my teachers and friends who have tried to educate me, and to those everywhere who value the pursuit of truth.

Contents

ix	**Acknowledgments**
xi	**A Plausible Fiction Masquerading as History**
xvii	**Introduction**
1	**Chapter 1**
	Jonah and Nahum: Myth and History

    Jonah 1
    Nahum 7
    Sources and Additional Reading 9

11	**Chapter 2**
	The Documentary Hypothesis

    Dating The Sources 26
    The Dating of P 26
    The Dating of J 27
    The Dating of E 32
    Dating the Deuteronomist 33
    Conclusion 33
    Sources and Additional Readings 35

37	**Chapter 3**
	Creation

    Day 37
    What do the words "Adam" and "Eve" mean? 47
    Did sin enter the world through Eve's action? 49
    If Eve is not responsible for evil, did J's God create evil? 50
    Why were Adam and Eve expelled from Eden? 52
    The Flood 57
    The Tower of Babel 66
    Final Comment on P's Creation Account in Genesis 1-2.4b 68
    Conclusion 69

Appendix I 70
Appendix II 72
Sources and Additional Readings 74

75   Chapter 4
Origin of the Israelites in Judea

The Flight 76
Wandering in the Wilderness 80
The Conquest 81
Critique: The Flight 85
Critique: Wandering in the Wilderness 88
Critique: The Conquest 90
The Pastoral Nomad Hypothesis 98
Critique 99
The Peasant Revolt Hypothesis 100
Critique 100
The Ruralization Hypothesis 101
Conclusion 105
The Single Exodus Model 106
The Double Exodus Model 108
Appendix III 110
Appendix IV 111
Sources and Additional Reading 114

117   Chapter 5
The Deuteronomist vs. Ahab

Conclusion 126
Sources and Additional Reading 129

131   Epilogue
133   Index

Acknowledgments

I did not consider returning to formal study at the University of Chicago's Divinity school until John Collins suggested it to me. John is one of the most respected scholars in Hebrew Bible/Old Testament studies in the world. His suggestion had more power than he could have imagined. I was fortunate to take three courses from John before he moved to Yale University Divinity School as Holmes Professor of Old Testament Criticism and Interpretation.

I am grateful to Ronald Hendel, Norma and Sam Dabby Professor of Hebrew Bible and Jewish Studies in the Department of Near Eastern Studies at the University of California, Berkley. I first encountered Ron at a seminar at Oxford where he lectured on Genesis and encouraged my interest. Ron has been generous in offering comments on both an early and late draft of this book. In both instances, his comments have been most helpful.

I am also indebted to Tikva Frymer-Kensky, a professor at the University of Chicago Divinity School, who taught me about the Mesopotamian origins of much that is in our Bible; and to David Schloen, an associate professor at the University of Chicago's Oriental Institute, who, as a Syrio-Palestinian archeologist, guided me through the archeological evidence that has revolutionized the history of the Bible.

There have been other classes and seminars with outstanding scholars too numerous to list that have played an important part in my education.

Richard Rosengarten, Dean of the Divinity School at Chicago, my academic advisor, has been helpful in choosing courses and providing good advice relevant to my studies.

Rabbi Herbert Bronstein, Senior Scholar and Rabbi Emeritus at North Shore Congregation Israel in Glencoe, Illinois, and Lecturer at nearby Lake Forest College, provided important comments on the chapter on Jonah.

I have depended on Patricia Ahearne-Kroll to check my material and advise me of current scholarly opinion on the issues I write about. Pat has logged many hours of research in an effort to protect me from errors of fact or omission. In this process she has effectively conducted an independent study seminar in Bible for me and has filled many holes in my knowledge. Her comments, corrections and suggested sources have been most welcome and have made this a more accurate book. Pat is teaching Hebrew Bible at the Department of Philosophy and Religion at North Carolina State University.

Readers should thank Kathryn T. S. Bass, Ph.D. In addition to grammatical corrections, her expertise has improved the quality and readability of this manuscript. Kathryn is an accomplished published poet, and an educator, copywriter, and marketing consultant. I am proud to add that she is also my daughter.

Many of the suggestions of both Pat Aherne-Kroll and Kathryn Bass, like the scholars I quote, have been reproduced in whole in the text.

It is likely that many of these scholars will disagree with portions of this book. None of these people, who have been so generous with their time and talent, have responsibility for the ultimate draft of this book.

I also thank Dr. Gordon L. Anderson, the publisher of Paragon House for his incisive suggestions on the book's structure and focus, and Paragon's Acquisitions Editor, Rosemary Yokoi for her kind and gentle handling of my inquires.

I have received support from the clergy and members of my church, St. Augustine's Episcopal Church in Wilmette, Illinois; and especially from Bill Heyck, Professor of History at Northwestern University.

My office assistant, Linda Bertelsen, has also been most helpful, which is significant since, as a person of firm and conservative faith, she has grave doubts about many of the conclusions I reach.

Finally, I could not have finished this book without the continued support and encouragement of my beloved wife and companion, Suzanne.

A Plausible Fiction Masquerading as History

It is a blisteringly hot afternoon about twenty-five centuries ago on the banks of the Kebar Canal near Nippur in Babylon. A group of religious leaders are about to meet; they will wrestle with the problem of how to keep their people from abandoning their Israelite identity and disappearing into an alien culture.

They are Israelite priests. They are meeting in the Israelite settlement of Tel-abib. Their people have been uprooted from their homes in Judah and taken to Babylon where they are forced to live. Their Temple—and most of their city of Jerusalem—has been destroyed by the Babylonian army. Both the priests and the people have time on their hands. The people use their time to mourn their fate and complain that they have been abandoned by their God, *YHWH*.[1] The priests will put their time to better use. They will create or edit what we now know as the *Torah*/Pentateuch and several other important books of the Bible.

These priests are meeting at a time of religious crisis. Like all Israelites, these men have based their faith on the belief that *YHWH* has chosen the Israelites to be his people. But recent historical events seem to belie their faith in *YHWH's* favor. Within the last 150 years, the two Israelite nations, the Northern Kingdom Israel, and the Southern Kingdom Judah, have been destroyed by two powerful enemies, the Assyrians and the Babylonians respectively.

Exiled in Babylon, the priests are faced with the difficult task of explaining the seeming abandonment of the people by their God. They must convince their followers—and themselves—that *YHWH* still loves them and cares about their future.

Among their various concerns, there is one immediate consensus: the Israelite traditions must be preserved in writing. Many of these stories' roots are 500 or more years old, and in the present instability, it is especially important that they not be lost.

---

1. Usually pronounced "Yahweh," but devout Jews may not pronounce the name of God and use "Adonai" instead.

- There is the story of creation, including God's creation of men and women (in Hebrew, *ha adam* = mankind).
- There are stories about a Patriarch called Abraham who traveled from far away to Israel at God's command.
- There are the stories of the exodus from Egypt and the receipt of the laws from *YHWH*.
- There are stories about a hero, David, and his wise son Solomon.
- There are also prophesies.

These particular traditions, and many others, are all well known and valued by the people. The priests agree that all of these stories and prophecies should be preserved although, in some cases, they should be edited to fit current circumstances.

Many of these stories are already written. Many are oral traditions. All the stories must be collected. The oral stories need to be written down. Difficult decisions are required about:

- what to keep and what to discard,
- which prophecies should be edited, and in what way, and
- what to do with stories that contradict each other. (One problem is that the contradictory stories come from different tribes and each variation is valued by a different tribe.)

The priests engage in lengthy and sometimes contentious discussions about each of these stories and each of these difficult issues. Consensus does not come easily. It takes time. Let us imagine this conversation twenty-five centuries ago.

A priest in a dark robe begins, saying what all have thought.

"In the creation story, does not *YHWH* tell *ha adam* (i.e., mankind) that he is to have dominion over all creation? No other god has told that to his people, not Baal, not Chemosh, not Marduk, no other god! If our God has given us dominion, why do we suffer?"

Another priest responds, thoughtfully.

"In the flood story, does not *YHWH* say that he is destroying mankind because of their lack of moral behavior? Has any other God ever been concerned about mankind's acceptable moral behavior? And, have not our people committed immoral acts offensive to *YHWH* by worshipping in the high places, erecting Asherahs, and worshipping the Queen of Heaven? Does not that justify *YHWH*'s sending the Babylonians to punish us?"

A bright, intense, young priest stands to object.

"But recall that *YHWH* told Moses on Mount Sinai that he is, 'a God merciful and gracious…and abounding in steadfast love and faithfulness, keeping steadfast love for the thousandth generation, forgiving iniquity and transgression and sin.' Does not that mean that *YHWH* will forgive us and return us to Jerusalem?"

Among the murmuring of voices, the "it must be so" is repeated by many.
Another priest says,

"I am heartened by *YHWH*'s promise to 'forgive iniquity and sin.' I believe that should give us and our people hope for the future of Israel."

This observation is met with amens from the entire group.
Slowly, a well respected priest, a scribe, rises with a new concern on his lips.

"I am not satisfied with our creation story. *YHWH* is righteous and pure. He would never make *ha adam* with his hands. He would never make the mistake of thinking an animal would be a suitable partner for *adam*. I am writing a new creation story with *Elohim* [another word for God] creating the world and *ha adam* by his word alone so that he is not sullied by direct contact with *ha adam*. Most importantly, I will have *Elohim* declare that his creation, including *ha adam*, is 'good.'

For *ha adam* must have been good if made by *Elohim*. Only we are to blame when *Elohim* observes that 'the inclination of the human heart is evil from youth' after the flood."

The priests encourage their venerated colleague to write this new creation story.

On the difficult problem of what to do about the stories of events that contradict each other, the priests eventually reach a consensus. They decide that the oral traditions that contradict each other are so popular among the different tribes of their people that they must be preserved as each tribe understands the story, with the contradictions among them intact. While this will make for awkward reading, it will keep the tribes happy.

But the priests must do more than work out the final form the stories and prophecies will take. They must explain why the Israelites have experienced the disasters that have befallen them.

The priests study and discuss the work of a school of theologians we now call the Deuteronomist (D) writing about fifty years before these meetings began. D explained the conquest of the Northern Kingdom, Israel, as a punishment enacted by *YHWH* against the kings of Israel, who permitted (perhaps even encouraged) the worship of other gods.

As an example, King Ahab married a Canaanite princess who worshipped Baal, and he even built a temple to Baal for her and her court. According to D, there were no good kings of Israel.

D's explanation of the loss of Israel might make sense, but how could the similar disaster that struck Judah be explained? After all, according to D, most of Judah's kings were faithful to *YHWH* and acceptable to him. They were able to find, however, that a few Judean kings were as bad as the kings of Israel, particularly Manasseh who reversed the policies of his revered father, Hezekiah, and allowed the same type of abominable worship which led to Israel's fall. They also turned to one of their fellow priests, Ezekiel, who was present in the meetings. He had been prophesying that *YHWH* had been angry with Judah because of Judah's rebellious nature and had promised divine punishment.

The priests had found a cause of Jerusalem's and the Temple's destruction they could accept.

Thus, this group of priests, now known as the Priestly Writer (P), after extensive consultation among themselves and with members of the D school, embraced D's explanation for Israel's destruction and followed their fellow priest Ezekiel's use of similar reasoning to explain Judah's demise. They also edited the work of several prophets so that they seemed to predict the fall of both Israel and Judah.

The priests had to deal with one more problem. D's material emphasized the necessity of worship only in the Temple in Jerusalem. But there was no Temple in Jerusalem in which to worship. It had been razed to the ground. The priests were relieved to find that Ezekiel had also prophesied that *YHWH* would lead them back to Jerusalem in a new Exodus and the Temple would be rebuilt. Thus, the question of worship and the Temple's destruction was finessed by the promise of a new Temple.

P had collected, organized, edited, and merged the old stories and prophecies with P's newly written material, including an explanation for the punishment *YHWH* had inflicted on Judah and the respected priest's new creation story. The resulting scrolls make up the backbone of the Hebrew Bible/Old Testament.

The Priestly Writers, P, succeeded. After the Persians under Cyrus conquered Babylon, the Israelites were permitted to return to Jerusalem with Cyrus providing funds to rebuild the Temple, as Ezekiel predicted. The scrolls so painstakingly created by the Priestly Writers were carried to Jerusalem and read to the people by Ezra so they could be proud of their origins, be aware of the sins that had caused their captivity in Babylonia, and become familiar with the extensive laws that would govern their lives. These laws included guidelines for treating neighbors, strangers, women, slaves, and children that formed a basis for similar laws and customs still present today in Western countries.

While some of these laws seem overly stringent today, those requiring compassion for the poor, justice for those without power, freedom from oppression, and respect for the property of others have survived in our laws and mores. Further, the concept of a god who has compassion and love for his people may be unique in the Ancient Near East (ANE), and survives in the Judeo-Christian world today. We will see these characteristics in Chapter 1 (on Jonah), Chapter 3 (on the creation), and Chapter 4 (the exodus).

This imagined scenario is a plausible rendering of what occurred in the final draft of two sections of the Bible (the *Torah*/Pentateuch and the Prophets) which were probably completed during the period of the Exile in the 6th century BCE.

Introduction

> "If you steal from one author, it's plagiarism; if you steal from many, it's research."
>
> —*Wilson Mizner*

Many of the ideas that form a foundation of our Western civilization are found in the Bible. They have developed, to be sure over 2,500 years, but the first big step was the final drafting of most of the Hebrew Bible around the time of the Exile in Babylonia in the 6th or 5th century BCE. The roots of the Bible stem from the Ancient Near East (ANE) and are at least 5,000 years old, extending back first to Egypt and Sumer, then, later, to Akkad, Mari, Babylonia, Assyria, Canaan, and many other areas in the ANE. Among other goals, this book identifies these roots as they influenced the writing of the books of the Bible discussed here, and identifies some of the breathtaking changes the biblical authors made in their creation myths, changes that revolutionized the way Israelites conceived of themselves and their relationship with God.

This book contains little if any original scholarship. But the research behind this book does borrow from the work of nearly fifty of the outstanding scholars in the fields of biblical studies and archaeology. By scholars, I mean teachers and researchers in academic environments not overly influenced by theological dogma. I believe I have generally presented as much of a scholarly consensus as can occur in these circles. A different group of scholars, in most cases a minority, will disagree with many of the conclusions in this book. That is the nature of scholars and scholarship. Certainty can be found only in faith.

This book consists of a series of essays that focus on the part of the Hebrew Bible/Old Testament concerned with events alleged to have occurred before the destruction of the First Temple in 587/6 BCE.[1]

As used in the title and elsewhere, Bible means what Jews call the Hebrew Bible and what Christians call the Old Testament.

There are footnotes and reading lists for those who wish to explore further.

---

1. Instead of the traditional BC and AD, I will use the more theologically neutral BCE (before Christian era) and CE (Christian era) except where BC/AD appear in quotations.

As used here,

History is the literary form that attempts to depict, in the words of the famous 19th century German historian, Leopold von Ranke, "what actually happened,"[2] and *Myth* is, "A traditional story, either wholly or partially fictitious, providing an explanation for or embodying a popular idea concerning some natural or social phenomenon or some religious belief or ritual; specifically, one involving supernatural persons, actions, or events."[3]

There are important truths in the early books of the Bible, however these truths are generally figurative and mythological. By and large, the history is biased and tells us more about the religious thought, politics, and culture of ancient Israel than, "what actually happened." While the religious thought, politics, and culture of ancient Israel is interesting to some scholars, only the mythological lessons of the Bible transcend time and are relevant to the lives of scholars and non-scholars alike in the 21st century. A good example of this is found in Chapter 1, on Jonah and Nahum. Jonah is clearly a myth but has a vital truth the author wants us to know. Nahum is very good history, but contains little if any lasting truth for us to ponder.

Consider the story about Joseph that completes the book of Genesis (Chapters 37-50). Was there an actual Joseph who lived that story? To this date, there is no attestation of that story in the available Egyptian records. The Joseph story may have its roots in two earlier Egyptian stories,[4] but, it does not make any difference whether or not it is historically true when we focus on the story's power. What could be a

---

2. von Ranke said he was writing history *"vie es eigentlich gewesen."* An alternate translation is "as it actually was." Most modern historians believe that is an impossible task, but I see no reason why we should not continue to try.

3. Lesley Brown, ed., *The New Shorter Oxford English Dictionary* (Oxford: Clarendon Press: 1993), Vol. 1, 1874.

4. George W. Coats, "Joseph, son of Jacob," in the *Anchor Bible Dictionary* (*ABD*), David Noel Freedman, et. al. eds. (New York: Doubleday: 1992) Vol. 3, 979. The "Tale of Two Brothers" contains a seductive scene similar to that between Potiphar's wife and Joseph in Gen. 39; and the "Tale of Sinuhe" tells of an Egyptian official who becomes successful in a foreign land, similar to Joseph's success in the court of the Pharaoh.

better depiction of the destructiveness of sibling rivalry, the strength of family ties, and the redemptive value of forgiveness? The Joseph story does tells us profound truths.

Most of the early Biblical stories have roots in ancient oral traditions and have been influenced by previous writings from Mesopotamia and elsewhere. In the Bible, however, the meanings conveyed within these stories have been (frequently and significantly) changed. These biblical story-myths conveyed truths important to the ancient Israelite community. Many of these truths, such as the value of compassion, love, and justice, are equally important to us today.

Another example of the combination of historical inaccuracy and mythological value is examined in Chapter 4. It is clear to archaeologists and the vast majority of biblical scholars (believers and non-believers alike) that the Israelites did not wander for forty years in the wilderness on their way from Egypt to the Promised Land. There is no extra-biblical support for this story—nothing in the extensive records from Egypt or elsewhere and not a shred of supporting archaeological evidence after extensive exploration in the areas quite clearly identified in the story. Chapter 4 reports this evidence in some detail. The mythological meaning, however, remains and is profound. The exodus story—from the flight from slavery in Egypt, through the wandering in the wilderness, to the conquest of the Promised Land—can be seen today as endorsing the importance of freedom for mankind, the importance of a safe place to live, and the author's (or authors') belief that God supports freedom and safety. These are values we still embrace today.

In general, the number 40 in the Bible simply means a long time. For example, the Israelites spent 40 years in the wilderness, it rained 40 days and nights to create the flood, and Moses was on the mountain for 40 days and 40 nights. Jesus spent 40 days in the wilderness. In all four cases the meaning is probably "a long time," not necessarily exactly 40 days or years.

The "40 years in the wilderness" story teaches that the pursuit of freedom and the search for a safe place to live are difficult, dangerous, and may take "40 years" (i.e., a long time). It is ironic that modern Israelis (as well as Palestinians) are relearning the truth of this myth about the difficult and dangerous struggle to find "a safe place to live" today, some 3,000 years later.

While this story may be best understood by Jews,[5] as a non-Jew I believe the story has a universal message for all of us, Jews, Christians, and all other peoples.

Many of us are not aware of the importance of genres in the Bible. It was common in the ANE to use well-known genres as frames for a writer's story, and it was recognized that the significance of the story did not stem from the elements of the genre but from the ideas that were, so to speak, hung on the genre. Ancient audiences were familiar and comfortable with common genres and expected authors to use them. If we look beyond the genre, we will find the wisdom intended by the author.[6]

Two examples detailed in Chapter 3 will illustrate:

First, the creation of man in the Adam and Eve story uses genres from many Mesopotamian myths. In these Mesopotamian myths, man was created to do the burdensome work previously done by the lesser gods. Man was essentially created to be a slave. In Genesis, man is created to have dominion over the earth—to be a partner of God, not a puppet. This was a dramatic break from previous understandings of mankind's place in the world, of mankind's importance, and of mankind's relationship with God. I believe this higher status for humans in Genesis 1 is reconfirmed in the rejection of slavery, at least for the Israelites in Egypt. Also, I believe the search for freedom and safety, found in the exodus story, still has a divine message for many of us today.

Second, the flood story in Genesis is part of the biblical creation myth and is an ancient genre. Geologists tell us that there has not been a flood that even covered the ANE (never mind the world) in the last several million years. Nevertheless, there are many flood stories in the Mesopotamian creation myths with elements surprisingly similar to the

---

5. See, e.g., Jon D. Levenson "Exodus and Liberation," in *The Hebrew Bible, the Old Testament, and Historical Criticism: Jews and Christians in Biblical Studies* (Louisville, KY: Westminster/John Knox Press: 1993), 127-159.

6. I use genre here as a literary model. The definition of genre in *The Random House Dictionary of the English Language,* 2nd ed. (New York: Random House: 1987) is, "a class or category of artistic endeavor having a particular form, content, technique, or the like." Also, Joel Marcus, "Mark 1-8" in ABD, 65, "a communication system, for the use of writers in writing, and readers and critics in reading and interpreting." Some biblical scholars have more technical definitions.

Noah flood story in Genesis. Many scholars believe that the wild and dangerous floods common to the Euphrates River were the inspiration for these Mesopotamian flood stories.[7]

In any event, these earlier flood stories created a genre for the writer of the Noah story to hang his tale on, and he did a skillful and creative job of using the genre to tell us how different early Israelite theology was from previous Mesopotamian theology. The problem is that most of us focus on the genre (i.e., the flood), and few of us have understood the important advance in theology that the story conveys. Chapter 3 provides the details.

Consequently, we should turn our focus from the elements of the genres to the truths conveyed by the myths. For example, we should not be preoccupied with looking for the remains of the ark because the evidence indicates that the story is a myth. We should not be preoccupied with trying to find the geographic location of Eden because evidence indicates that also is a myth. Instead, we should concentrate on what the authors believed about our role in the universe, our responsibilities to others, and our relationship to God. If we look beyond the genre, we will find the wisdom intended by the author.

Mere shadows of history may endure in the oral traditions about Abraham and Moses. On the other hand, David and Solomon are certainly historical figures. But the stories about these heroes have probably been exaggerated or fabricated to aggrandize them, and the historical accuracy of many of the stories has been compromised. Similarly, in spite of our more rigorous demands for historical accuracy today, we have exaggerated the exploits and character of our heroes (e.g., George Washington and Abraham Lincoln); the accuracy of some of the popular stories about them is similarly compromised.

The books 1 and 2 Kings tell us of the period from David's death and the ascension of King Solomon to the Babylonian destruction of Jerusalem over 350 years later in 587/6 BCE. These books read like history, and, in some respects, they can be called historical books. However, they were written in Judah and Babylon by authors completely convinced that the

---

7. Most biblical and oral tradition scholars do not support the theory that the break in the natural dam between the Mediterranean and Black Seas in c. 5000 BCE contributed to the oral tradition that gave rise to the flood genre.

destruction of Israel, completed in 721 BCE, was caused by Israel's sins against God. In 2 Kings 17.7f, we read,

> This occurred because the people of Israel had sinned against the Lord their God, who had brought them up out of the land of Egypt from under the hand of Pharaoh, king of Egypt. They had worshiped other Gods and walked in the customs of the nations whom the Lord drove out before the people of Israel, and in the customs that the kings of Israel had introduced. The people of Israel secretly did things that were not right against the Lord their God.

I believe that, to the contrary, the cause of Israel's and Judah's destruction was twofold:

a. Israel and Judah practiced unfortunate foreign policy: Both plotted with the Egyptians to resist empires to whom they had pledged loyalty and were obliged to pay homage, Israel to the Assyrians and Judah to the Babylonians. Egypt provided no help for either Israel nor Judah. The Assyrians and the Babylonians, quite predictably, punished Israel and Judah (which revolted even after Egypt had been defeated by the Babylonians) for this treachery.
b. They were no match for the overwhelmingly superior military force of the avenging Assyrians and Babylonians.

Israel's and Judah's religious practices almost certainly had nothing to do with their defeat.

Thus, much of the history we do read in the Bible is written to glorify biblical heroes or to advance a decidedly theological point of view.

Ultimately, the myths in the Bible, however historically inaccurate, are worth pondering. In the words of Ronald Hendel, concerning many of the Bible's myths, "Even if it didn't happen, it's a true story."[8]

Most of the biblical quotations used here are from the New Revised Standard Version. Where it seems indicated, I will also quote from the Jewish Publication Society version.

---

8. Ronald Hendel, *Bible Review*, (June, 2003), 8.

Chapter 1

Jonah and Nahum: Myth and History

The books of Jonah and Nahum are short; a little over two and three pages respectively in the *New Oxford Annotated Bible, New Standard Revised Edition*, (NOAB). They each address the same topic, God's actions with respect to Israel's hated enemy, Assyria, but they could not be more different in tone and in moral message.

Jonah

In a comment before the book of Jonah in the NOAB, Jonah is described as "an obscure Galilean prophet from Gath-hepher who counseled Jeroboam II (786–746 B.C.)," but it is unlikely that this is the same Jonah of this story. Almost all scholars agree that the Book of Jonah was not written by the 8th century prophet, Jonah. Most scholars believe it was written sometime between the 6th and 4th centuries.[1] In other words, at or after the Priestly Writers were finishing their work on Genesis through 2 Kings.

The Book of Jonah is based on "older material from the realm of popular legend,"[2] and was originally in two parts, Chapters 1–2 and Chapters 3–4.

Here is a brief outline on the first part, presented in Chapters 1 and 2.

- Jonah is told by God to "arise" and go to Ninevah (capital of the hated Assyrians) and prophesy its destruction.

---

1. R. Lansing Hicks and Walter Brueggemann, "Jonah," *The New Oxford Annotated Bible* (NOAB) New Revised Standard Version, eds, Bruce M. Metzger and E. Roland Murphy (New York: Oxford University Press: 1991), 1186, OT. Also, David Jones "Jonah, Book of" the *Anchor Bible Dictionary* (ABD) eds. David Noel Freedman, et. al. (New York: Doubleday: 1991), Vol. 3. 940-1. See 2 King 14.25.

2. NOAB, 1186, OT.

- Jonah does "arise," but instead of going to Ninevah, he flees in the opposite direction on a ship headed for Tarshish,[3] thought of then as the other end of the world—and as far away from the God of Israel as Jonah can imagine.
- A great storm ensues, threatening the ship and the lives of its pagan crew and its passenger, Jonah.
- The crew casts lots and determines that Jonah has somehow caused the storm. They question him, and he admits that the cause of the storm is his fleeing from God.
- Although the crew hopes to save Jonah's life, they fail to overcome the storm. Praying, "Please, O Lord…do not make us guilty of innocent blood; for you…have done as it pleased you," they throw a willing Jonah overboard, offer a sacrifice to God (*Elohim*, not their local god) and hope for forgiveness. The storm immediately ceases.
- Jonah is swallowed by a great fish.
- He composes and recites a psalm-like prayer, praising God and promising to sacrifice to God, presumably in the temple in Jerusalem, indicating his willingness to return to Israel and be prepared to do God's will.
- After three days and three nights, "the Lord spoke to the fish, and it spewed Jonah out upon the dry land."[4]

---

3. Richard Fletcher, *Moorish Spain*, (Berkley, Los Angeles: University of California Press: 1992-3), 86. "Jonah…had taken ship for its (the Guadalquivir River's) famous trading port Tarshish (or Tartessos)," located on the Atlantic Ocean side of modern Spain. However, Baker, David W., in ABD, Vol. VI, 931 states, " its exact location is still a matter of debate."

4. In 1 Corinthians 15.3f, Paul wrote, Christ "was raised on the third day in accordance with the scriptures." These words were incorporated into the Nicene Creed. The scriptures referred to must have been from the Hebrew Bible, since Mark, the first Gospel, was written about twenty years after Paul's death. This passage from Jonah is one of the candidates for this distinction. Jonah's rescue after three days in the belly of the fish, is possibly echoed in Jesus' resurrection on the "3rd day," in both the Apostles and Nicene creeds. The phrase in Jonah 2.6, "I went down to the land whose bars closed upon me forever; yet you brought up my life from the Pit," is, perhaps, echoed in the Apostles Creed, written many centuries after Jonah but before the Nicene Creed, "He descended into hell; the third day he rose again from the dead."

Chapters 1 and 2 carry an important message to us. God forgave Jonah's disobedience after he repented.[5]

There is no indication in the text that Jonah was a professional prophet—that is, a Prophet usually trained at court to prophesy for the king and other important government and religious figures.[6] In all the other prophetic books, there are pages of eloquent prophecy. However, in Jonah, there are only five simple and direct Hebrew words constituting the book's entire prophecy (translated on the next page).[7]

Why does Jonah flee? Not because he is afraid for his personal safety. Rather, he is afraid God will not destroy Ninevah. In chapter 4, verse 2, Jonah tells God,

"That is why I fled to Tarshish…you are a gracious God and merciful, slow to anger, and abounding in steadfast love, and ready to relent from punishing."[8]

---

5. In Jonah 1.9, Jonah confesses his commitment to God by saying, I am a Hebrew…I worship the God of heaven." This follows 1.2 where the word of the Lord says to Jonah, "Go at once to Ninevah…"

6. In a Midrash [biblical exegesis (analysis)] probably dated 100-300 CE ("Mekhilta D'Rabbi Ishmael" vol. BO), the rabbis noted there were three different kinds of prophets or religious teachers: prophets only concerned with the will of God, like Elijah; prophets who were universalists, i.e., interested in God's concern with justice and compassion for all peoples, like Jeremiah (and Amos, Isaiah, and many others); and, prophets who were radical particularists like Jonah who was only interested in the welfare of the Jews. Jonah thought that if Ninevah repented and was saved, it would be bad for the Israelites. Professional (court-centered) prophets, like Amaziah in Amos 7.10, ceased to exist centuries earlier before this Midrash was written.

7. This simple prophecy leads some scholars to question whether this Jonah was a prophet or simply a believer that was given this one-time prophetic charge. But, in the story, Jonah's prophecy is very successful, suggesting divine approval. Also, Amos received a single call to prophesy, and no one questions Amos' credentials as a prophet.

8. In Exodus 34.6-7 on Mt. Sinai, the Lord proclaimed himself to be, "The Lord, a god merciful and gracious, slow to anger, and abounding in steadfast love…forgiving iniquity and transgression," and in Numbers 14.18 Moses reminded God of God's own statement that, "The Lord is slow to anger, and abounding in steadfast love, forgiving iniquity and transgression." Perhaps the memory of these biblical passages is behind Jonah's words, recalling God's weakness—compassion. Similar language occurs in other biblical books.

Jonah was only interested in the welfare of the Israelites, and he was horrified at the thought of prophesying to Ninevah, the capitol of Assyria, Israel's most dangerous enemy. Instead of warning them that God would soon destroy them, Jonah would have preferred God to simply proceed with the destruction. His fears that Ninevah would heed the prophecy would come to pass as we will see in the second section, Chapters 3 and 4.

Here is a brief outline on the second part, presented in Chapters 3 and 4.

- Jonah is again told by God to "arise" and go to Ninevah and prophesy its destruction.
- This time, Jonah does "arise" and go to Ninevah; and he prophesies its destruction in five Hebrew words, translated as "forty days more, and Ninevah shall be overthrown."
- To Jonah's horror, the Assyrian king believes the prophecy and orders that, "Human beings and animals shall be covered with sackcloth, and they shall cry mightily to God [Elohim, not an Assyrian god]…so that we do not perish."[9]
- God "relents" and spares Ninevah.
- Jonah is angry with God for sparing the hated Assyrians.
- Jonah wishes to die, and sits in the burning sun.
- God causes a plant to grow to give Jonah shade.
- God destroys the plant.
- Jonah has compassion for the plant and cries out to God.
- God points out that as Jonah has compassion for the plant, God has compassion for all mankind, even Ninevah.

Notice how the author's portrayal of a contentious Jonah adds to the story's power.

---

9. Jonah 3.8-9. The animals cry out to God? This unbelievable phrase lends some credibility to belief that the story of Jonah is a satire. See James S. Ackerman, "Jonah" in *The Literary Guide to the Bible*, Robert Alter and Frank Kermode, eds. (Cambridge, MA: Harvard University Press, 1987), 239, 242.

Also, notice the parallels between Chapters 1 and 2 and Chapters 3 and 4:

Chapters 1 and 2	**Chapters 3 and 4**
• The crew of the ship is pagan.	• The Ninevites are pagan.
• Nevertheless, they pray to a universal (not their own) god.	• Nevertheless, they pray to a universal (not their own) god.
• After Jonah prays (repents), God has compassion and saves Jonah.	• After the Ninevites pray (repent), God has compassion and saves the Ninevites.

Is the Jonah story historically accurate? "Until the modern period, the historicity of the book, at least among Christians, seems to have been taken for granted."[10] Modern scholarship finds it difficult to accept the historicity of a man living in "the belly of the fish three days and three nights." While acknowledging that with God all things are possible, it is hard to believe that anyone could live in such an acidic environment with neither oxygen nor potable water. Also, research has been unable to find a period when the aggressive, militant, cruel, and expansionist Assyrian Empire repented and stopped their murderous incursions against their neighbors. Thus, this story lacks historical credibility. It is a parable (a form of myth). It may also be, according to Ackerman (see footnote 9 on page 4), a satire; or, as we will see later, a might-have-been. It is interesting to note that Jews generally do not see the story as historic, because rabbis in the early centuries identified it as a parable with an important message.

Jonah teaches an important Judeo-Christian lesson:

> While God is just, he also has love and compassion for all peoples, and he is always willing to forgive those that repent, even non-Israelites.

---

10. Jonathon Magonet, "Jonah, Book of," ABD, Vol. 3, 940.

This restates Exodus 34.6-7 while adding non-Israelites to those to whom it applies. It confirms the message, new to the ANE, that God cares about people, a message that still resonates throughout Western civilization and has become an integral part of our understanding of God and ourselves. The lessons about God's forgiveness for those who repent are sufficiently profound to render the historical accuracy issue irrelevant.

Would pages of prophecy have prepared us better for the message of Chapters 3 and 4 than did Jonah's five Hebrew words? Probably not. No one has to puzzle over the meaning of this prophesy. The terse precision and clear words of Jonah's prophecy were the most effective way of prodding Assyria to repentance, resulting in God's forgiveness.

All of Jonah is read in Synagogue in the afternoon service of *Yom Kippur*, the Jewish Day of Atonement. The liturgical calendar in Christian churches calls for the reading of passages from Jonah. In those readings, Jews and Christians relearn that God's love was (and is) not just for his people, the Israelites (and Jews),[11] but is universal: a powerful lesson in such a short book.

Jonah also teaches us that a story does not have to be historically accurate to be true. We will see this same point confirmed again and again in the following chapters.

A final and incredible note on Jonah. "Early every Thursday morning from [the years] 1594 to 1599 [George Abbot, future Archbishop of Canterbury] preached a sermon on a part of the Book of Jonah. That is 260 Thursdays devoted to a book [which] is precisely four chapters long, a total of forty-eight verses. Abbot devoted over five sermons to each of them.[12]

Nahum

The Bible is filled with contrasting viewpoints, and this chapter would be incomplete without considering the following passages from arguably

---

11. The Israelites were not called Jews until the Persian Period in the 5th century BCE, about the time the book of Jonah was written.

12. Adam Nicolson, *God's Secretaries* (New York: HarperCollins Publishers: 2003), 157.

the most universally ignored book of the Bible, the Book of Nahum:

> 1.1 An oracle concerning Nineveh. The book of the vision of Nahum of Elkosh. A jealous and avenging God is the Lord, the Lord is avenging and wrathful; the Lord takes vengeance on his adversaries and rages against his enemies. The Lord is slow to anger but great in power, and the Lord will by no means clear the guilty.
>
> 2.13…I will burn your chariots in smoke, and the sword shall devour your young lions…and the voice of your messengers shall be heard no more.
>
> 3.5 I…will lift up your skirts over your face; and I will let the nations look on your nakedness and kingdoms on your shame. I will throw filth at you and treat you with contempt, and make you a spectacle. Then all who see you will shrink from you and say, "Nineveh is devastated; who will bemoan her?" Where shall I seek comforters for you?
>
> 3.19 There is no assuaging your hurt, your wound is mortal. All who hear the news about you clap their hands over you. For who has ever escaped your endless cruelty?

These verses celebrate the destruction of Nineveh in 612 BCE by the Medes (who later became part of the Persian empire) and the Babylonians. "The date of Nahum's triumphal ode lies close to the event it foretells,"[13] probably sometime between 612 BCE and the first successful siege of Jerusalem in 597/6 BCE by the Babylonians, an event that would have caused the author of Nahum to be far from enthusiastic about the Babylonians (the second and total destruction of Jerusalem occurred 10 years later in 587/6 BCE). Nahum portrays the region's understandable relief and joy at Assyria's destruction, and the book clearly indicates the widespread terror caused by Assyria's almost annual campaigns in the region. Nahum is more accurate history than Jonah.

It is interesting that Jonah was written after Nahum and the destruction of Nineveh. This suggests that the author of Jonah may have

---

13. NOAB, 1200.

wondered if Nineveh might have been spared if it had been willing to repent and change its ways.

But Nahum, while part of the Bible, is not included in Christian Lectionaries,[14] and is not read in Jewish worship services. In contrast, Jonah is included in Christian Lectionaries, and plays a prominent role in the Yom Kippur service, the most holy day in the Jewish calendar.

While Nahum's portrayal of the fate of Ninevah in the late 7th century BCE is more historically accurate, Jonah's lessons, though mythological, have endured to play a significant role in the Judeo-Christian understanding of man's relationship to God.

---

14. A book of biblical passages read on a certain day in religious services.

Sources and Additional Reading

Ackerman, James S. "Jonah" In *The Literary Guide to the Bible*, ed. Robert Alter and Frank Kermode. (Cambridge: Harvard University Press: 1987), 234–243.

Fletcher, Richard. *Moorish Spain*. (Berkley: University of California Press: 1992–3).

R. Lansing Hicks and Walter Brueggemann, "Jonah," *The New Oxford Annotated Bible* (NOAB) New Revised Standard Version, eds., Bruce M. Metzger and E. Roland Murphy. (New York: Oxford University Press: 1991).

Magonet, Jonathon, "Jonah, Book of," *The Anchor Bible Dictionary*, (ABD), eds. David Noel Freedman, et. al., (New York: Doubleday: 1991), Vol. 3.

Chapter 2

The Documentary Hypothesis

The first five books of the Bible—Genesis, Exodus, Leviticus, Numbers, and Deuteronomy—are called the *Torah*[1] by Jews and the Pentateuch by Christians. Beginning in the 17th century, serious readers of the Bible began to comment on the "numerous duplications, a broad diversity of style, and contrasting viewpoints" evident in these books.[2]

The Documentary Hypothesis had its beginnings with "Richard Simon (1638-1712), who argued that the Pentateuch had been compiled from a number of documents...Jean Astruc (1684-1766) claimed there were two sources, one that used *Elohim* and the other, *YHWH*"[3] as the Hebrew name of God." Scholars refined the theory of sources until a consensus was reached in the mid 19th century that identified the four sources we now refer to as P (Priestly Writer), J (Yahwist), E (Elohist), and D (Deuteronomist).

The theory of the Documentary Hypothesis is that these five books were largely the work of these four sources. The identification of P, J, and E passages used in this chapter is the work of Martin Noth.[4] D is the author of almost all of Deuteronomy. Later, the books of Joshua, Judges, 1 and 2 Samuel, and 1 and 2 Kings were also attributed to D. Evidence leading scholars to distinguish these four sources includes:

- differences in literary style,
- differences in language usage (including the different name of God),

---

1. *Torah* is an anglicized rendition of the Hebrew word for the first five books of the Bible. Other italicized words in this chapter will be similar renditions of the appropriate Hebrew word.

2. Antony F. Campbell and Mark A. O'Brien, *Sources of the Pentateuch* (Minneapolis: Fortress Press: 1993), 1.

3. Usually pronounced "Yahweh," but devout Jews may not pronounce the name of God and use "Adonai" instead.

4. Ibid., 19.

- differences in theology and other viewpoints, and
- duplication of narrative.

For example, in Chapter 3, and later in this Chapter, we will see the differences in literary style and language between P's creation story in Genesis 1 and J's in Genesis 2-4; and, we will see their theological differences regarding the nature of God. Their duplicate narrative contributions in the subsequent flood story (with important differences) also confirms separate authorship.

It would be a mistake to imagine four individual authors. Although some of J's work in Genesis (e.g., the Adam and Eve story) and some of P's work (e.g., the Genesis 1 creation story) may have come from a single author, it is probable that the balance of the sources are predominantly collaborations from various contributors from each school of P, J, E, and D who wrote, rewrote, and redacted (edited) these texts over several centuries.

It would also be a mistake to assume there is general consensus among scholars on the nature of these sources, the number of times the sources were redacted, and by whom, and the order and date of each source. There are also a minority of scholars who dispute the existence of these sources, believing instead that the *Torah*/Pentateuch is made up of many fragments of oral tradition that were patched together by a redactor.[5]

For our purposes here, however, we will adopt the belief of the majority and assume the general validity of the Documentary Hypothesis while recognizing that it may take many forms. What follows is a discussion of each of the sources.

The *Priestly Writer* (P) is responsible for most of the genealogies, laws, and regulations. P is best known as the author of Genesis 1.1 through 2.4a, the story of the creation "of the heavens and the earth" in six days, with God resting on the seventh. P writes like a lawyer, i.e., terse and to the point. Certainly, much of P's writing in Leviticus is formal, dry, legal dictum. But we should also note that P's creation narrative in Genesis 1 is quite poetic and beautiful.

P's God is transcendental (i.e., distant from man, way up there), omniscient (i.e., all knowing), and omnipotent (i.e., all powerful). You

---

5. For a brief discussion of the "Fragment Hypothesis" see Campbell and O'Brien, 3.

will see later in this chapter that J's God is very different.

P refers to God as Elohim (God, in English translations) until his passage in Exodus 6 (similar to E's Exodus 3) where God finally identifies himself to Moses as *YHWH* (the four sacred Hebrew letters of God's name never to be pronounced by devout Jews, who say "Adonai" instead of "Yahwey," which is usually used by others, and is a closer rendering of the Hebrew). After P's Exodus 6.2, where God reveals his name to Moses, P refers to God as *YHWH* (Lord, in English translations).

One of P's major theological contributions is the "evisceration of the demonic… [P] posits the existence of one supreme God who contends neither with a higher realm nor with competing peers. The world of demons is abolished.…With the demise of the demons, only one creature remains with 'demonic' power—the human being."[6] P believed that human "moral and ritual sins" had the power to drive God out of his sanctuary. "All that the priests can do is periodically purge the sanctuary of its impurities and influence the people to atone for their wrongs."[7]

Thus, the P school, quite logically given the above assumption, concerned itself with purity, dietary, and other laws, and rituals for almost every conceivable occasion. Impurity itself is not serious as long as purification is not delayed so long that the "impurity affects the sanctuary,"[8] which adversely affects the entire community including the innocent and the virtuous. Thus, the Priestly Writer believed that the entire community could suffer as a result of one person's sins, and that there was no individual reward for virtue.[9]

---

6. Jacob Milgrom, "Priestly Source" in *The Anchor Bible Dictionary* (ABD) David Noel Freeman, et.al., eds. (New York, et.al.: Doubleday: 1992), Vol. 5, 454.

7. Ibid., 455. But Jon D. Levenson argues in *Creation and the Persistence of Evil*, that God only limits chaos, and that P's cultic life of Israel imitates this divine act; i, e., prevents chaos from taking over.

8. Ibid.

9. But Ezekiel 18 (dated early 6th century BCE, perhaps at P's time) states, "If a man is righteous…he shall live." In the Hellenistic period of the 3rd and 2nd centuries BCE, we find a belief in an afterlife with God. An example is in 4 Maccabees 9.8, the story of the seven brothers who refused a tyrant's orders to violate the dietary laws. They say to the tyrant before being tortured to death, "For we, through this severe suffering and endurance, shall have the prize of virtue and shall be with God on whose account we suffer."

This transference of demonic power from semi-divine creatures to human beings resulted from P's determined monotheism, which rendered demons unthinkable and impossible. Since the culture had been so imbued with the idea of demons and their power, the effect of demonic power could not be ignored. In the absence of demons or any other semi-divine power, humans were the only possible carriers of that power.[10]

Today, most Judeo-Christian theologians differ from P in that they do not believe our transgressions affect God, only the transgressor.

Through biblical times, up until surprisingly late, many people thought there was a large body of water over the dome of the sky. In the creation story, in Genesis 1.6, P wrote,

> "And God said, 'Let there be a dome in the midst of the waters, and let it separate the waters from the waters.' So God made the dome and separated the waters that were under the dome [i.e., the waters on and under the earth] from the waters that were above the dome. And it was so. God called the dome Sky."

Thus, P, and most Israelite contemporaries, as well as Jews and Christians through the Middle Ages, believed there was a substantial body of water above the sky in addition to the water on and under the earth.

Therefore, P described the beginning of the flood in Genesis 7.11,

> "All the fountains of the great deep [i.e., water on and under the earth] burst forth, and the windows of the heavens [i.e., the water above the sky] were opened."

J's description of the origin of the floodwaters is different, as you will note later.

P was writing for "a specific audience around the time of Israel's exile.[11] P believed "God set the world in motion in the majestic splendor of

---

10. P's goal to eliminate the "world of demons" in Israelite culture obviously failed for millennia. In the 1st century CE, according to the New Testament, Jesus contends with demons in many passages; and until recent centuries, most people believed in devils/demons. Many people still believe in the Devil today.

11. The exile in Babylon began with the conquest of Jerusalem in 597/6 BCE, and accelerated with the destruction of Jerusalem in 587/6 BCE.

the creation account, crowned by God's Sabbath which, of all the world, only Israel observed. God's purpose would not fail. God set Israel on the march toward the promised land, splendidly and majestically organized around the sanctuary of God's presence to the people. God's purpose would not fail. Individuals may fail and be replaced…[but] God's purpose would not fail."[12] To place this in context, in J's creation account, humankind (*ha adam*) was expelled from the garden (did the people see this as a metaphor for Israel's exile to Babylon?) and sent east (Babylon is east of Jerusalem), never to return to Eden. Thus, P's accounts offered a hope sorely needed to those returning from exile, those in exile, or those about to go into exile.

"The Priestly document is a powerful affirmation of faith in God's unconditional commitment to Israel which, although delayed by human frailty, will never be deflected from the ultimate goal of God's love."[13]

The school of P may have originated in Bethel in the Northern Kingdom of Israel and migrated to Jerusalem, encountering another "priestly tradition, that of the school of the Holiness Code (H)…In the final stages of the priestly composition the two literary traditions—P and H—were joined."[14] We will continue to refer to this school as P.

The P school is credited with being the major influence in the Torah/Pentateuch, almost universally recognized as a major participant in various redactions (editings), including the final one. Rofè describes this redaction graphically. He states that the priestly school, "seized control of the literature which modern research has labeled JE [Yahwist and Elohist], the rich literature that preceded them and that described history from the first man until Moses, and they edited it comprehensively, whether by short additions at the beginning or end of the accounts, or by adding entire stories which completely change the nature of the composition…[for example P's] account of creation in Gen. 1.1-2.4a which wholly contradicts the older [Adam and Eve] story in 2.4b-3.24."

---

12. Campbell and O'Brien, 21; assumes P wrote around the time of the exile.

13. Ibid., 22.

14. Alexander Rofè, *Introduction to the Composition of the Pentateuch* (Sheffield: Sheffield Academic Press: 1999), 134. The Holiness Code is found in Lev. 17-26.

Rofè also points to the oration of Moses at the end of Deuteronomy (32.48-52) in which he discloses the details of his own death which is "unmistakably priestly in style."[15]

The *Yahwist* (J) is best known as the author of the Adam and Eve story; an older and a quite different creation story than P's.

The name J originated with German scholars because J refers to God as *YHWH* (usually pronounced "Yahwey" and translated into English as Lord). J is the first letter of *YHWH* in German; Jehovah is a word for God derived from *YHWH*.

Unlike P, J most certainly did not write like a lawyer. J was a great story teller and used a freer, more narrative style than P. If J were alive today he (or perhaps the entire school) would be a popular and successful writer.

Most scholars believe J's sources were older oral traditions from various areas and tribes. If that is true, J skillfully wove these disparate traditions into his narrative.

J's contribution in Genesis is more than twice that of E, and more than three times that of P. D has no contribution in Genesis, other than possibly, along with P, that of a redactor.

J's God is very different from P's God. While P's God is transcendental, omniscient, and omnipotent; J's God, while he may be omnipotent, is far from transcendental, that is to say, he is hardly distant from humans:

- He formed Adam from the ground and breathed life into him (Gen. 2.7).
- He created the animals in Adam's presence for him to appraise (Gen. 2.19).
- He made Eve from Adam (Gen. 2.22).
- He walked in the garden (Gen. 3.8).
- He made clothes for Adam and Eve (Gen. 3.20).
- He talked to Noah and his sons after the flood (Gen. 9).
- He took "ethical instruction from Abraham" (Gen. 18.22-33).[16]

---

15. Ibid., 134.
16. Ronald S. Hendel, "Genesis, Book of", ABD, Vol. 2, 934.

P's God would never interact with humans in this way.

Also, J's God is certainly not omniscient. That is, J's God seemed to be surprised by events as they unfolded. For example,

- God forgot to prohibit Adam from eating of the Tree of Life when he prohibited eating of the tree of the knowledge of good and evil. Later, God realized the danger that Adam may eat of the Tree of Life and become "like one of us," and expelled Adam from Eden.
- At first, God apparently thought an animal would be an appropriate "companion" for Adam, and only when Adam rejected all animals for this role, did God create Eve. Incidentally, this tension before Eve is finally created makes compelling reading and is an example of J's literary skill.

P's God would know all events before they occurred and would never be surprised.

There are two other interesting distinguishing features of J's God. In Genesis 6.5-7, in an introduction to the flood story, God decided to "blot out from the earth the human beings I have created"…because, "the wickedness of humankind was great in the earth." Then, after the flood, in Genesis 8.21, he tells Noah that even though "the inclination of the human heart is evil from youth…I will [n]ever again destroy every living creature as I have done." Note that human nature has not changed, it is God that has changed. We also see God change what will trigger his destruction of Sodom and Gomorrah in his encounter with Abraham in Genesis 18.

In contrast, P's, and as we will see, D's God is eternally perfect. It would never occur to either of those schools that their God would change his mind or his policy.

A minor contrast between P and J occurs during the flood story. P's description of the flood in Genesis 7.11 refers to the water above the dome of the sky, "fountains of the great deep burst forth and the windows of heavens were opened" [from the large body of water over the dome of the sky]. In contrast, J wrote in Genesis 7.12 only that, "The rain fell on the earth forty days and forty nights." J, at least, identifies "the waters above the dome" as rain.

The *Elohist* (E) wrote from a northern perspective; i.e., from Israel, not Judah.[17] E's material is both the shortest of the sources and the most controversial. While there is consensus on the existence of P, J, and D, there is controversy on whether there was,

1. a discrete E narrative, or
2. an E which is only a collection of varying traditions of J's, or
3. a collection of independent fragments pasted into the Pentateuch by a redactor.

Like P, E refers to God as Elohim; but, unlike P, E continues to call God Elohim even after God reveals his name as *YHWH* in E's text in Exodus 3 (similar to P's Exodus 6).

We will assume the existence of a discrete E source whose work was probably severely edited and cut before the Pentateuch was finalized. We will also assume that E's principal source was J. There is substantial evidence to support this hypothesis. "E is represented in every major segment of the Pentateuchal traditions:

- the promises to the fathers (e.g., Gen. 15.1-6),
- Moses and the exodus from Egypt,
- the Sinai [E's Horeb] covenant,
- the wilderness wandering,
- the Balaam oracles, and
- the end of Moses' life after he transfers his authority to Joshua."[18]

---

17. Alan W. Jenks ("*Elohist*," ABD, Vol. 2, 481-2), points out E's "emphasis on northern sites such as Bethel and the similarities between E's vocabulary [e.g., E refers to 'Horab' rather than 'Sinai'] and the characteristic vocabulary of Deuteronomy [originally from the North]...E shares significant theological themes...with Deuteronomy and Hosea [a northern prophet of the 8th century]." and with the Samuel and Elijah traditions as well," [both clearly northern prophets], all very concerned with idolatry and the potential misuse of power by kings. But see possible effects of redaction on page 32.

18. Ibid., 479, 480. In addition to the "major segments" above, E also is responsible for the testing of Abraham/binding of Isaac story and E is a major contributor to the Joseph story.

"This sketch of E's contents lends weight to the belief that E, prior to its being combined with J, was an independent narrative strand stemming from a northern version of…the common epic tradition of the pre-monarchial period."[19]

The major characteristics of E are:

1. Prophetic leadership: Abraham, Jacob, Joseph, and Moses are idealized and "their forceful prophetic leadership is counterposed to the power of kings;"
2. The fear of God: "Several significant E passages are linked together by the repeated mention of the fear of God;"
3. Covenant: "The centerpiece of E's theology of history is the covenant of Israel with God at Mt. Horeb ('Sinai' in the J and P traditions);" and
4. Theology of History; unlike P or J, E is concerned only with the history of Israel beginning with Abraham.[20]

As previously stated, other scholars believe E is nothing but a fragmentary variant of J. It is difficult to see E as a variant of J, since what tentatively identifies E is frequently a correction of J, more or less presenting a more acceptable version of the story in J. Further, E's material often goes "beyond J in one way or another…For example, E's version of the Jacob-Esau stories has a passive Jacob, the victim of Laban's disfavor, rather than a cunningly active Jacob accumulating wealth and envy" as portrayed by J (Gen 30-31). On Jacob's return, E's Esau is actively welcoming and accepting (Gen. 33.4-5, 8-11), in contrast to the suspicious and grudging Esau of J (Gen. 33.12-16)"[21]

We must revisit J in this section because of the apparent interaction between J and E. It seems apparent that one of E's goals is to sanitize J.

As one example, consider J's version of a well-known story in Genesis, Chapter 12.[22]

---

19. Ibid., 480.
20. Ibid., 480-481 for all four characteristics.
21. Campbell and O'Brien, 162.
22. Ibid., 99.

"Now there was a famine in the land. So Abram [he became Abraham later] went down to Egypt to reside there as an alien, for the famine was severe in the land. When he was about to enter Egypt, he said to his wife Sarai [she became Sarah later], 'I know well that you are a woman beautiful in appearance; and when the Egyptians see you, they will say, This is his wife; then they will kill me, but will let you live. Say you are my sister, so that it may go well with me because of you, and my life may be spared on your account.' When Abram entered Egypt the Egyptians saw that the woman was very beautiful. When the officials of Pharaoh saw her, they praised her to Pharaoh. And the woman was taken into Pharaoh's house. And for her sake he dealt well with Abram; and he had sheep, female donkeys, and camels. But the Lord afflicted Pharaoh and his house with great plagues because of Sarai, Abram's wife. So Pharaoh called Abram, and said, 'What is this you have done with me? Why did you not tell me that she was your wife? Why did you say, She is my sister, So that I took her for my wife? Now then, here is your wife, take her, and be gone.' And Pharaoh gave his men orders concerning him; and they set him on his way, with his wife and all that he had."

In J's version of this story,

- Abram lies about his relationship with Sarai.
- The story, as written, suggests that Pharaoh had sex with Sarai.
- God intervenes indirectly by sending plagues, and we are left wondering how the Pharaoh connected them to his relationship with Sarai, because it is not clear in the text.

Also, J endangers the genealogy so vital to the story of Israelite beginnings by putting Sarai in Pharaoh's control. It may explain the subsequent name change to Sarah, and her bearing Isaac in her extreme old age, many decades after the events in this Chapter 12 story, which would put to rest any possibility that Pharaoh was Isaac's father.

Incidentally, this device by J adds tension and interest to the story, making our reading of it more pleasurable. There is an interesting anachronism in J's story. J has Pharaoh giving Abram camels. Camels were not in general use until the end of Iron Age 1, about 1000 BCE, while the story time of the Abram/Abraham stories is probably Middle Bronze Age, before 1550 BCE.

There is a similar story attributed to E in Genesis Chapter 20:

"While residing in Gerar as an alien, Abraham said of his wife Sarah, 'She is my sister.' And King Abimelech of Gerar sent and took Sarah. But God came to Abimelech in a dream by night, and said to him, 'You are about to die because of the woman whom you have taken; for she is a married woman.' Now Abimelech had not approached her; so he said, 'Lord will you destroy an innocent people? Did he not himself say to me, 'She is my sister?' And she herself said, He is my brother. I did this in the integrity of my heart and the innocence of my hands.' Then God said to him in the dream, 'Yes, I know that you did this in the integrity of your heart; furthermore it was I who kept you from sinning against me. Therefore, I did not let you touch her. Now then, return the man's wife; for he is a prophet, and he will pray for you, and you shall live. But if you do not restore her, know that you will surely die, you and all that are yours.' So Abimelech rose early in the morning, and called all his servants and told them all these things; and the men were very much afraid. Then Abimelech called Abraham, and said to him, 'What have you done to us? How have I sinned against you, that you have brought such great guilt on me and my kingdom? You have done things to me that ought not to be done.' And Abimelech said to Abraham, 'What were you thinking of, that you did this thing?' Abraham said, 'I did it because I thought, There is no fear of God at all in this place, and they will kill me because of my wife. Besides, she is indeed my sister, the daughter of my father but not the daughter of my mother; and she became my wife. And when God caused me to wander from my father's house, I said to her, This is a kindness you must do me; at every place to which we come, say of me, He is my brother.' Then Abimelech took sheep and oxen, and male and female slaves, and gave them to Abraham, and restored his wife Sarah to him. Abimelech said, 'My land is before you; settle where it pleases you.' To Sarah he said, 'Look, I have given your brother a thousand pieces of silver; it is your exoneration before all who are with you; you are completely vindicated.' Then Abraham prayed to God; and God healed Abimelech, and also healed his wife and female slaves so that they bore children."

This seems to be a reaction to J's story in Genesis 12, not a variant or an independent fragment. While J's story in Genesis 12 appears to have oral roots, E's story here seems to be a written commentary on J's story.[23] E clearly sanitizes J's story, maintaining his idealization of Abraham, as evidenced in the following observations:

- Notice how E absolves Abraham from lying to Abimelech by identifying Sarah as his sister as well as his wife.
- Notice how careful E is here to be sure the reader knows that Abimelech did not have sex with Sarah, eliminating the concerns raised in J's account of the same story in Genesis 12 using a different cast of characters and keeping her safe from possibly contaminating the genealogy, and.
- Notice how E provides the answer to how the king/Pharaoh knew that Sarah/Sarai was Abraham's/Abram's wife by having God tell him that in a dream.
- Notice how E omits camels from the gifts to Abraham, perhaps an example of E cleaning up J's anachronism.

In confirmation of E's idealization of Abraham and others, Ronald Hendel writes, "In E's narratives, beginning with Abraham in Genesis 20, the human protagonists are often idealized, with their deceits and ambiguous acts explicitly justified [i.e., sanitized]…God's role in the stories is much more pronounced than in J."[24]

There is a third similar story in Genesis Chapter 26 surprisingly attributed to J:

> "Now there was a famine in the land, besides the former famine that had occurred in the days of Abraham. And Isaac went to Gerar, to King Abimelech of the Philistines. The Lord appeared to Isaac and said, 'Do not go down to Egypt; settle in the land that I will show you. Reside

---

23. John Van Setters, *Abraham in History and Tradition* (New Haven: Yale University Press: 1975), 173. And, Claus Westermann, *Genesis 12-36*, (Minneapolis: Fortress Press: 1995), 318–319.
24. Hendel, 934.

in this land as an alien...' So Isaac settled in Gerar. When the men of the place asked him about his wife, he said, 'She is my sister;' for he was afraid to say, 'My wife,' thinking, 'or else the men of the place might kill me for the sake of Rebekah, because she is attractive in appearance.' When Isaac had been there a long time, King Abimelech of the Philistines looked out of his window and saw him fondling his wife Rebekah. So Abimelech called for Isaac, and said, 'So she is your wife! Why then did you say, she is my sister?' Isaac said to him, 'Because I might die because of her.' Abimelech said, 'What is this you have done to us? One of the people might easily have lain with your wife, and you would have brought guilt upon us.' So Abimelech warned all the people, saying, 'Whoever touches this man or his wife shall be put to death.'"

1. Notice that the opening phrase is identical to the opening of the similar story of J's in Genesis, Chapter 12, and the rest of the sentence refers to an earlier story.
2. Notice that the location, Gerar, and the king, Abimelech; identical to E's location and king in Genesis, Chapter 20. No scholar or archaeologist to date has been able to locate Gerar, and there is no record of a King Abimelech (it may be an indication of kingship like Pharaoh in Egyptian).
3. Why is there no sexual threat to the line from Isaac as there is in J's story about Abram? Perhaps J did not want to defer the birth of Jacob and Esau to assure the purity of the line, as he had to do with Abraham and Sarah.
4. Is it possible that one purpose of these three stories is to establish that the patriarchs had very attractive wives, which may have been evidence of their power and of God's approval of them?

These three stories in Genesis 12, 20, and 26 are known as the "ancestress in danger" stories because of the threat to the genealogical line. An analysis of them suggests that E and J may have been contemporaries who read and reacted to each other. This theory sees the chronology of the three stories as,
    a. J's Abram and Sarai in Egypt.

b. E's Abraham and Sarah in Gerar (E sanitizes J).

c. J's Isaac and Rebekah in Gerar (J simplifies E's story).

An alternative theory would have E's Abraham and Sarah in Gerar story written after both J stories and that E only needed to sanitize J's Abram and Sarai in Egypt story since J's Isaac and Rebekah story did not need sanitizing.

It seems to me more likely that J wrote his second story in response to E's story. Why would J write a second similar story? He does not repeat his stories anywhere else in the Bible.

The *Deuteronomist* (D) is the author of Deuteronomy. The D school has also been credited with the books of Joshua, Judges, 1 and 2 Samuel, and 1 and 2 Kings. These books are referred to as the Deuteronomistic History (DtrH). D calls God, *YHWH* (D's writings all occur after God reveals his name in Exodus 3/6). The DtrH writers concerns were moral exhortation, social justice, and historiography (writing history through the prism of their theology). The fingerprints of D and DtrH include these factors:

- God is of the whole world;
- Israel is a treasure;
- Everything Canaanite is evil;
- God is transcendental (therefore, sacrifice is not as important since God neither eats nor smells);
- Sermons;
- Separation from foreigners: no intermarrying, no treaties with foreign lands;
- The relationship with *YHWH* is one of intense love on both sides;
- Worship is centralized in Jerusalem; and
- D is more concerned with family laws than P is (as expressed in Exodus), therefore limiting somewhat the absolute authority of the father.[25]

---

25. Class notes, "Ancient Israelite Religion" Winter Quarter, 2001, Divinity School, University of Chicago, Tikva Frymer-Kensky and David Schloen.

The DtrH consistently glorifies the Southern Kingdom, Judah, over the Northern Kingdom, Israel. DtrH blames Israel's fall on lack of ritual and religious purity that became an obsession in Judah under kings Hezekiah (727-698 BCE) and Josiah (639-609 BCE). There were fewer non-Israelites in Judah than in Israel,[26] so uniform purity of religious observance was more attainable. But the kingdom of Israel had large Canaanite and Aramean populations, and the kings of Israel allowed those peoples to worship their own gods. This was interpreted as idolatrous by the religious powers in Judah, including the school of D who joined in the attack on this alleged idolatry in their former country.[27]

In 1 Kings 6, D inserts a warning to Solomon to mend his ways, which seems to explain the split of the unified monarchy in the 10th century BCE; but, more subtly, this passage explains the destruction of the Northern Kingdom, Israel, in the 8th century BCE by the Assyrians. YHWH warned Solomon:

> "If you turn aside from following me, you or your children, and do not keep my commandments and my statutes that I have set before you, but go and serve other gods, and worship them, then I will cut Israel off from the land that I have given them and the house that I have consecrated for my name I will cast out of my sight; and Israel will become a proverb and a taunt among all peoples."

Chapter 4, "The Origin of the Israelites," will include the evidence that the biblical version of the Exodus, the Wandering, and the Conquest is a myth and is not history (i.e., "what actually happened"). In the DtrH, D picks up the story in the wilderness and carries it through the Conquest, the stories of David and Solomon, and those of the kings of Judah (the Southern Kingdom) and Israel (the Northern Kingdom)

---

26. Scholars disagree on how many non-Israelites were in Judah at this time. Some say there were very few, but others point to the aggressive policies of Hezekiah to rid Judah of polytheistic practices suggesting a larger non-Israelite population; but that may also indicate polytheistic practices by the Israelite population.

27. McKenzie, Steven L., "Deuteronomistic History, ABD Vol. 2, 162, "… ancient traditions were preserved…by northern prophetic circles. After the devastation of Israel in 721 B.C.E, members of these circles fled S[outh] to Judah with the traditions they had collected…[and] threw their support behind Hezekiah's doomed reform[s]."

until the Exile. The DtrH presents an idealized picture of Joshua's conquest (the evidence is presented in Chapter 4), and probably also idealized David and Solomon, emphasizing the support they had from *YHWH*. Thus, J's and E's writings in the books of Exodus and Numbers had to be edited to conform to the DtrH.

Dating The Sources

Dating the sources is difficult. Scholars, like detectives, use various clues to develop theories about when they were written. There is some, but not much, consensus about exactly when the writing took place. The following probably represents the view of many if not most scholars. Keep in mind that most of the material was composed and redacted by long-lived schools. It is likely that parts of many sections of the *Torah*/Pentateuch were written and redacted in different periods. There is much more material here on the dating of J than any of the other sources. That is because the J material illustrates more clearly how scholars go about creating their theories on dating.

The Dating of P

An early debate concerned the dating of P. The most prominent scholar who clearly laid out the Documentary Hypothesis, and temporarily closed the debate on the dating of P, was Julius Wellhausen. His late 19th work, *Prolegomena to the History of Ancient Israel*,[28] argued for a late date. Today, about half of the scholars prefer a late date; generally thought to be during or after the exile, i.e., the 6th or 5th century BCE. The other half prefer an earlier, pre-exilic date. It may be they are both right. Hendel writes, "It appears that the P source is best described as a collection of independent narratives and as a redactional source. It may be that this implies more than one compositional phase for P, perhaps a pre-exilic P writer and an exilic P redactor."[29]

---

28. Originally published in 1878 as *History of Ancient Israel*. The *Prolegomena…*was an 1883 reprint.

29. Hendel, 934.

The Dating of J

J wrote earlier than P. But we do not know how much earlier. The dating of J is currently in dispute. There is good evidence for dating J in either the 10th or the 7th centuries BCE, or somewhere in-between. Until recent years, it was the consensus among scholars that J wrote in the 10th century BCE in the court of King Solomon, allegedly the first time in Israelite history that extensive literary work would have been encouraged. Solomon's empire was thought to have been large and rich; and establishing its origins, heroes, and justification would have been a priority. This consensus has now been challenged by younger scholars. Here are both arguments:

Arguments for a 10th century dating of J

1. The treaty between Jacob (from Israel) and Laban (from Aram),[30] as related by J in Genesis 31.51-54, containing the injunction that Laban (Aram), "...will not pass beyond this heap and this pillar to me, for harm." The well known German scholar Hermann Gunkel believed this could not have been written after 860 BCE (the wars between Israel and Aram are dated 860-779), because, "The redactor (of J) did not dream that the Syrians (Arameans) would one day break out in rage against Israel and dismember it."[31]

   Supporters of a 7th century dating respond by pointing out that the Jacob/Laban story does include substantial hostility and mutual suspicion. This rebuttal does not match the strength of Gunkel's argument. In fact it is quite possible to turn the rebuttal on its head by suggesting that a 7th century redactor was the one who inserted the "substantial hostility and mutual suspicion" into J's text.

2. The J material contains,

   • no allusions to the substantial Assyrian perils,[32] which, like the Aramean perils, began in the 9th century BCE.

---

30. Aram and the Arameans were located approximately in modern Syria.
31. Hermann Gunkel, *Water for a Thirsty Land* (Minneapolis: Fortress Press: 2001), 63.
32. The Assyrians were located approximately in modern northern Iraq.

- no hint of the division between Israel and Judah, a monumental event generally thought to have occurred in the late 10th century BCE.

3. Further, the cursing of Canaan in J's Genesis 9.25 reflects the political situation in the united monarchical period, as does J's Genesis 15.18; 25.23; 27.37, 40a; and J's Numbers 24.15-19.[33] These passages are concerned with subjugating Canaan, an issue of much less importance by the 7th century BCE.

4. While those proposing a 7th century dating of J include in their argument that Solomon's kingdom was quite modest, there is some evidence to the contrary. We will see in Appendix III of Chapter 3 the archaeological evidence of a large population in Judah about fifty years before Solomon. The area may have been rural but could have been relatively wealthy. Further, it is well documented that the Egyptian Pharaoh Sheshonq I (Biblical Shishak) campaigned against Judah and Israel in about 930 BCE, and was bought off by the Judaean King Rehoboam (Solomon's son) with enough riches to satisfy Sheshonq I. One scholar writes, "So rich was the tribute exacted that Sheshonq I could reopen the Gebel Silsilah quarries and add a court in front of the second Ramesside pylon at Karnak Temple."[34]

5. Some scholars believe there is a gross tendency for earlier myths to focus on creation, as J does, and later myths to focus on redemption, as does the DtrH and the 8th and 7th century prophets.

6. E, as we saw earlier, presents a Northern Kingdom point of view writing against J's Southern Kingdom point of view. If E is either J's contemporary, or postdates J, J could not have been a 7th century author since E's north fell to Assyria in the 8th century BCE.

These are impressive reasons to date J in the 10th century BCE.

---

33. Geneva de Pury, "Yawist (J) Source," ABD, Vol. 6, 1015.

34. Frank J Yurco, "Egypt and the Bible." Page 1 of an introduction to a course given at The Oriental Institute at the University of Chicago, Fall, 2002.

What appears to be a substantial proof of a 10th century J is his description of the borders of Israel promised to Abraham in Genesis 15.18-20, which are similar to the borders of Israel in Solomon's rule as described in 1 Kings 20 by D. But this is no longer as powerful an argument as once thought, since this description is explained by proponents of a 7th century BCE dating as a 7th century idealization of David and Solomon by D.

Rebutting those who believe in a very late J, Hendel noted that "The depictions of a sympathetic side of Esau (Edom) in J and E[35] are strong evidence against an exilic or post exilic [i.e., after 587 BCE] date for J [or E]; at this later time Edom was reviled for its part in the sack of Judah"[36] Further, in Amos 1.11, Edom is cursed, "because he pursued his brother with a sword and cast off all pity." Although Amos is dated to the middle of the 8th century, many scholars believe this was a later exilic addition.

Arguments for a 7th century dating of J.

1. Many of the sites J writes about in the Exodus story were not in existence in the story time of the Exodus. Many were not developed until the 7th century. Some were developed only in the 7th century. Moab, Edom, and Ammon on the Transjordan Plateau were "very sparsely inhabited in the Late Bronze Age [1550-1200 BC]. In fact, most parts of this region, including Edom, which is mentioned as a state ruled by a king in the biblical narrative, were not even inhabited by a sedentary population at that time…there were no kings of Edom for the Israelites to meet." Edom "reached statehood only under Assyrian auspices in the seventh century…before it was a sparsely settled fringe area inhabited mainly by pastoral nomads."[37]

   Kadesh-barnea, where the Israelites allegedly camped for thirty-eight of the forty years of wandering, yielded no evidence of any

---

35. See J in Genesis 27.30-38, and E in Genesis 33.4-16.

36. Hendel, 934, referring to Ps 137:7; Obadiah; cf. Ezekiel 25.12-14; Isaiah 34.5-17; 63.1-6; Malachi 1.2-4.

37. Israel Finkelstein and Neil Silberman, *The Bible Unearthed* (New York: The Free Press: 2001), 64, 68. See Numbers 20.19.

settlement in the Late Bronze Age, but a 7th century fort has been found there.[38]

2. J's Numbers 21 tells of the attack against the Israelites by the king of Arad. But there have been no Late Bronze Age artifacts recovered from Tel Arad.[39]

3. In conflict with those who believe in the biblical report of the wealth of Solomon's empire, some archaeologists and biblical scholars have raised serious doubts about Solomon's empire. No archaeological evidence of his palace or temple has been unearthed (in fairness, local regulations make it very difficult to dig in Jerusalem) and structures elsewhere in Palestine originally attributed to him have been re-dated by some archaeologists to the work of subsequent kings of the Northern Kingdom, Israel. Israel is known to have been a more powerful and wealthy kingdom in the 9th through most of the 8th centuries BCE than Judah, the Southern Kingdom, the seat of the house of David. The kingships of David and Solomon are alleged by these scholars to have been minor fiefdoms in an overwhelmingly rural and poor area. These archaeologists and scholars now suggest that the biblical description of Solomon's empire is an idealized view of Judah's past, composed 300 years later, in the 7th century, when Judah was finally attaining true statehood after the final destruction of the Northern Kingdom, Israel, in 721 BCE by the Assyrians, and the large increase in population in Judah with the influx of refugees from Israel.[40]

Camels were not in general use until about 1000 BCE. Would a J writing only about eighty years later assume that camels were in general use several hundred years earlier in Abraham's time? Either J was unaware of how recent the use of camels was, or this becomes another piece of evidence supporting a later J.

---

38. Ibid., 63.
39. Ibid., 64.
40. Ibid., 230.

What appears to be a substantial proof of a 7th century J is the fact that none of the prophets writing before the exile seem to know about the Adam and Eve, the Cain and Abel, or the flood stories. But, supporters of a 10th century dating respond that a late date is not persuasive, since: "…chapters 1-11 of Genesis must be regarded as a separate element of the Pentateuch, that is, as a relatively self contained unity, and not primarily as a part of Genesis."[41] This rebuttal is credible because Genesis 1-11 deals with humanity as a whole in its primordial origins and is not focused on the story of Israel's origins. The balance of the *Torah/Pentateuch*, and indeed the rest of the Hebrew Bible/Old Testament, focuses on Israel's origins, its history, and its relationship with *YHWH*. Therefore, there is no reason why it should refer back to the Primordial events in Genesis 1-11, since they have nothing to do with Israel's story. Further, J himself does not refer back to Adam and Eve, Cain and Abel, or the flood after the beginning of the Abraham cycles.

It is clear that legitimate confusion on the dating of J—and persuasive arguments for both a 10th and 7th century BCE J—will persist until further evidence emerges.

I believe that J's original draft in Genesis was written in the 10th century BCE, but his account was redacted later to add elements of hostility between Israel and Aram that history had already verified. The redactor also added stories of the 'Wandering in the Wilderness" that fit the political geography of the 7th century BCE. The Deuteronomist, D, and even more so the Priestly Writer, P, then heavily redacted the rest of J's writings to conform to their vision of Hebrew history and myth. D had a powerful presence in 7th century King Josiah's court, and P was a dominating force during and after the Exile some one hundred years later. They certainly had the power to redact J, and they would have thought it justified by their religious beliefs. Having idealized David and Solomon, they also may have wanted to idealize Moses by redacting J's Exodus story.

According to D and P, Moses was able to prevail against the Pharaoh and the powerful Egyptian army (with what would have been an untrained

---

41. Claus Westermann, *Genesis 1-11*, trans. by John J. Scullion S.J.(Minneapolis: Fortress Press: 1994), 2.

group of nomads), only with the help of *YHWH*. To illustrate this emphasis of D on the necessity of *YHWH's* support, recall D's story of Saul in 1 Samuel 31, who, after losing *YHWH's* support, lost an important battle with the Canaanites during which both he and his sons were killed.

J's creation stories in Genesis 2—11 may well have escaped 7th century redaction and may be close to the original early writing of J since those chapters do not deal directly with either the history of Israel or Judaean 7th century theology. But both J's and E's writings in the rest of Genesis and all of Exodus and Numbers were probably heavily redacted to conform to D's, and later P's, theology.

The Dating of E

The dating of E is also in dispute. As stated earlier, there is good evidence dating J in either the 10th or the 7th Centuries BCE. E's dating has been suggested in the 10th, 9th, and 8th centuries BCE. As previously stated in footnote 17 on page 18, E shares theological views with D and the prophet Hosea, and it had been suggested that E wrote in the 8th century, matching the time of D and Hosea. "From the originally proposed 8th-century date, scholarly opinion has shifted…to an earlier date. One proposal has been that E should be dated to the late 10th century… More commonly proposed…is the 9th century."[42] For the reasons outlined on pages 23 and 24, I tend to believe E to be roughly contemporary with J, making E, perhaps, a late 10th century author.[43]

As with J, we must also expect that the D redactors made significant changes in the E material in the 7th century to conform to D's theology; thus, much of E conforms to the theological views of D and Hosea. Scholars who believe the E material is only the work of a redactor (perhaps D) who assembled older oral fragments would date the E material in the 7th or 6th century.

---

42. Jenks, 482.

43. A later E must assume that the Isaac/Rebekah story was the work of a later, different J than the J of the Abram/Sarai story.

Dating the Deuteronomist

The story of the discovery of "the book of the law" in 2 Kings 22.8 is identified with the 18th year of Josiah's reign, which occurred in either 622 or 621 BCE. Many scholars believe this "book of the law" was the first draft of D's book of Deuteronomy. The school of D went on to produce the DtrH, the books of Deuteronomy, Joshua, Judges, Samuel 1 and 2, and Kings 1 and 2. There is also evidence of the D school's influence in Jeremiah and elsewhere.[44]

Conclusion

It seems that there are at least four discrete authors or schools of authors in the books of Genesis, Exodus, Numbers, Leviticus, and Deuteronomy. While E may be only a collection of fragments woven into the P and J accounts by a redactor, one can make a persuasive case that, in any event, some kind of an E has at least taken oral fragments and converted them to a written form using a distinct style, a distinct language, and expressing a distinct viewpoint. In either event, E is an important contributor to the Pentateuch.

The words of Rofè provide an appropriate, if somewhat complex, conclusion:

> "…the composition of the Pentateuch [along with the rest of the DtrH] appears to have been a lengthy and complex process, lasting from the days of the Judges until the end of the Persian period—in other words, from the twelfth century until the fourth century BCE, a period of approximately eight hundred years. This process included all of the stages of composition—initial oral transmission, commitment of individual stories to writing, composition of cycles of stories and collections of laws, compilation of these types of compositions as they underwent editing, and finally the addition of new, late-originated, works to the existing platform…The Pentateuch thus can be seen as

---

44. Rofè, 133.

a combination of the compositions of three defined schools—D, H[45] and P—that operated between the seventh century and the fourth century BCE and worked over the remnants of the rich literature that preceded them, that is, the literature that it was customary to refer to in the past by the sigla J and E. Two theological tractates—the Deuteronomic and the Priestly—supplied…the theological principles of the Pentateuch."[46]

If we view the Documentary Hypothesis as an outline of authorial sources with many areas of uncertainty that future scholarship will slowly resolve, we will be much closer to the truth than we would be adopting a fixed sense of authorship.

This is only an introduction to the Documentary Hypothesis and the controversies surrounding it. A full treatment of all of the currently considered alternatives and adjustments to the basic theory would extend to thousands of pages, and, unfortunately, would result in little additional clarity.

---

45. The school of the Holiness Code that merged with P, see page 15.
46. Rofè, 130, 135.

Sources and Additional Readings

Campbell, Antony F. and O'Brien, Mark, *Sources of the Pentateuch* (Minneapolis: Fortress Press: 1993).

de Pury, Geneva, "Yahwist ("J") Source," in *The Anchor Bible Dictionary* (ABD) David Noel Freeman, et. al., eds. (New York: Doubleday: 1992), Vol. 6.

Gunkel, Hermann, *Water for a Thirsty Land* (Minneapolis: Fortress Press: 2001).

Hendel, Ronald S., "Genesis, Book of," in ABD, Vol. 2.

Jenks, Alan W., "Elohist," in ABD, Vol. 2.

Levenson, Jon, *"Creation and the Persistence of Evil: the Jewish Drama of Divine Omnipotence* (Princeton, NJ: Princeton University Press: 1994)

McKenzie, Steven L., "Deuteronomistic History," in ABD, Vol. 2.

Milgrom, Jacob, "Priestly Source," in ABD, Vol. 5.

Rofè, Alexander, *Introduction to the Composition of the Pentateuch* (Sheffield: Sheffield Academic Press: 1999)

Setters, John Van, *Abraham in History and Tradition* (New Haven: Yale University Press: 1975).

Westermann, Claus, *Genesis 1-11*, trans. by John J. Scullion S.J. (Minneapolis: Fortress Press: 1994).

Westermann, Claus, *Genesis 12–36*, trans. by John J. Scullion S.J. (Minneapolis: Fortress Press: 1995).

Chapter 3

Creation

In Genesis Chapter 1, heaven and earth are created in six days with God resting on the 7th day. The order is as follows:

Day

1. God created light, day and night (the darkness was already there).
2. God created the sky, which separated the waters under and over the sky.
3. God gathered the waters into seas,—separating out the "dry land"—and created plants and trees.
4. God created the sun, moon, and stars.
5. God created fish and birds.
6. God created first animals, and then "humankind in our image."

In Chapter 2, verse 2, the author, P (the Priestly writer), states, "And on the seventh day God finished the work that he had done, and he rested…" While this account is beautiful and poetic, it is also terse and tightly written. As stated in the previous chapter, it does read like something a lawyer would write, and P, a priest, was trained in the law contained in that portion of the *Torah*/Pentateuch written before his work and the oral or written traditions behind his own work.

Recall from Chapter 2 that P refers to God as *Elohim* (translated into English as God), because P believed the name *YHWH* was not available to the Israelites until it was revealed to Moses in Midian in P's Exodus 6: "I am the Lord [*YHWH*]. I appeared to Abraham, Isaac and Jacob as God Almighty. But by my name, 'The Lord' I did not make myself be known to them."

P's *Elohim* creates entirely *by his word alone.* This is probably why the New Testament Gospel of John opens with, "In the beginning was the word…" P's God is transcendental, omnipotent, and omniscient (i.e., very distant, all-powerful, and all knowing).

Scholars debate the dating of P. Many believe Genesis 1 was written sometime after 596 BCE during the exile of the Israelites in Babylon or during the post-exilic period toward the end of the 6th or in the early 5th century BCE. Others believe P was written earlier.

Following P's account is J's Adam and Eve in Eden story, which may be the best known story in the Judeo-Christian world. It begins at Genesis 2.4b and continues to the end of Chapter 3. It is a seemingly simple story; the outlines are known to most of our older children. Nevertheless, in reality, it is very rich, most complex, and filled with ambivalence, enigmas, and seeming contradictions.

Here is an outline of the Adam and Eve story:

- The Lord God made, "the earth and the heavens…[and] formed Adam from the dust of the ground, and breathed into his nostrils the breath of life."
- Next, "the Lord God planted a garden in Eden…and made to grow every tree [including] the tree of life…and the tree of the knowledge of good and evil."
- "The Lord God…put the man in the Garden of Eden to till it and keep it."
- He then forbade Adam to eat of the tree of the knowledge of good and evil.
- He decided to make Adam a "helper as his partner," so he created the animals, "out of the ground," but Adam rejected them all.
- He then created "woman" out of Adam to be his partner.
- The serpent induced "woman" to eat the fruit from the forbidden tree; and she "gave some to her husband, who was with her, and he ate." (See page 48 for J's first use of the name "Eve.")
- They then became aware they were naked and made loincloths for themselves.
- The "Lord God" discovered their disobedience and cursed and punished the serpent; punished, but did not curse, Adam and

"woman"; and banished them from the garden to keep them from eating of the tree of life so they would not "live forever."

P was an ultimate editor of earlier authors and would not have approved of J's God who walked around and talked to Adam and "woman." P might have eliminated these and other observations reflecting on his belief in God's nature if J's writings had not been well known and widely accepted.

Many scholars believe the Adam and Eve story came from two older oral traditions. The first tradition may be the creation of Adam, the animals, and Eve and the paradise story in Chapter 2. The subject in Chapter 2 is predominantly God. The second tradition may be the transgression and expulsion story of Chapter 3. The subjects in Chapter 3 are predominantly Adam, Eve, and the serpent. In further support of the two source theory, in Chapter 2, God tells Adam he will die if he eats the forbidden fruit, but, in Chapter 3, Adam eats the fruit, and does not die, suggesting some disconnection between the two Chapters. We will see another piece of supporting evidence later.

J may have selected these two oral traditions out of many, and, with his usual narrative skill, united them, inconsistencies notwithstanding.[1]

Note the differences in the P and J creation stories other than P's *Elohim* and J's *YHWH*:

1. There is a wide difference in literary style.
2. J has *YHWH* create the earth and the heavens in one day; P uses days one, two, four and part of three for the same purpose.
3. J has *YHWH* create man before the animals; P reverses the process.
4. J has *YHWH* create the animals and man out of the ground; P has *Elohim* create them by his word.
5. P claims his story starts "In the beginning," J makes no such claim.
6. P and J have quite different ideas about the nature of God.

---

1. Claus Westermann *Genesis 1-11* (Minneapolis: Fortress Press: 1994) 187–190, surveys a variety of two-source theories. It is clear there is no consensus on the theory in general or on what verses in Genesis 2 belong to which tradition.

How could anyone doubt that these stories are from different authors? Yet, for well over 2,000 years, virtually all readers of the Bible believed that both of these stories were written by the same person, Moses. "From the time of its promulgation under Ezra and Nehemiah, (c. 500 BCE) the full *Torah* was regarded as having been composed by Moses."[2] It was only in the 17th century CE that a few readers of the Bible began to suggest there might have been more than one author. This is a clear example of the power tradition can hold over reason.

One of the important messages in Genesis is that, since P and J had very different ideas about the nature of God, and since both were acceptable to the compilers of the Bible, different ideas about God should also be acceptable to those honoring the Bible today.

While P and J differ in their portrayal of God, neither would think of God as only a creator. That is not even a concept that would have occurred to them. Their god is a god of action in the world, not a philosophical product of human thought.

Creation myths in Genesis continue after the Adam and Eve story with,

- J's account of Cain and Abel in Chapter 4, verses 1—24;
- a fragmentary genealogy in verses 25—26 assigned by Westermann to J,[3] but considered as unknown origin by Campbell and O'Brien;[4]
- P's genealogy from Adam to Noah in Chapter 5;
- a mixed J and P flood story in Chapters 6—10;
- J's Tower of Babel story in Chapter 11, verses 1-9; and ends with
- P's genealogy from Noah's son, Shem, to Abram—the Israelite patriarch—in Chapter 11, verses 10 through 26.

---

2. Richard Elliott Friedman, "Torah (Pentatuech)," *The Anchor Bible Dictionary* (ABD) (David Noel Freedman, et. al., eds. (New York: Doubleday: 1992), Vol. 6, 618. Also see *Nehemiah* 9.1, 10.29, 13.1.

3. Westermann, p. 326.

4. Antony F. Campbell and Mark A. O'Brien, *Sources of the Pentateuch* (Fortress Press: Minn.: 1993), 195.

There are also snippets of creation myths where God conquered chaos monsters in the Psalms, Job, Isaiah, Jeremiah, Ezekiel, and Amos. The chaos monsters have various identities: Rahab, Leviathan, Behemoth, dragon, serpent, and monsters.[5] These myths are generally older traditions than those in Genesis 1 through 11, and are, for the most part, direct descendants of previous Canaanite myths. They also parallel most Mesopotamian creation myths, which often use combat with creatures of chaos as agents of creation.

Myth and History are different. History is not the past, it is an attempted account of the past. History is fixed in time and is always *then*. History is also, according to von Ranke, *what actually happened*. It attempts accuracy, but has little if any universal truth to convey. History questions, challenges, and checks <u>all</u> sources. History is always tentative.

Myth is timeless and symbolic; it attempts to convey universal truths important to its community. Myth chooses its sources, ignoring others; its principal goal is inspiration, not accuracy. Myth is unquestioned and final.[6]

All creation myths involve divine action, and tell us of primordial time, which has no relationship to temporal time. That is, these myths cannot be fixed on any calendar or dated at a specific time. For us, the truths conveyed by our creation myths were true then, are true now, and will be true in the future. As William Faulkner said, "The past is never dead, it is not even past."[7]

Symbols are one-word tools used in myths.[8] For example, as we will see, Adam and Eve are each symbols of humanity; the serpent is a symbol of temptation.

---

5. Rahab in Psalms 87.4, 89.10; Job 9.13, 26.12; Isaiah 51.9. Leviathan in Isaiah 27.1; Psalms 74.14, and 104.26; Job 3.8 and 41.1. Behemoth in Job 40.15. Dragon in Psalm 74.13; Isaiah 51.9, and 27.1; Ezekiel 29.3; 32.2; Job 7.12. Serpent in Amos 9.3; Is 27.1; Job 26.13; Monster in Jeremiah 51.34.

6. See Ken Cameron "Rigor Without Mortis," *The American Fly Fisherman*, vol. 28, No 1, 19 for a discussion of history Vs myth in fly fishing. See also page x in the Introduction re history and myth.

7. William Faulkner, *Requiem for a Nun*, (New York: New York: Random House: 1951), 92. Ronald Hendel first brought this quote to my attention in a seminar at Oxford University in August, 1999.

8. Many biblical scholars hold to the "one-word tool" definition of symbols, but in philosophical circles, symbols can be more complex; e.g., they may be entire systems—like myths themselves.

Many of the sources of P's and J's creation accounts are found in Sumerian, Akkadian, and Babylonian creation myths dating from the 3rd and 2nd Millenniums BCE. These cultures, along with others, are called Mesopotamian. Three of the many myths from which biblical myths of the creation are formed are:

- *The Gilgamesh Epic*, a myth written in Akkadian with Sumerian sources and many versions. This Epic probably originated before 2000 BCE, at least 1,000 years before J's Adam and Eve story. In *Gilgamesh*, there is a plant that restores to youth those who eat it, similar to the Tree of Life in J's account. Also a serpent who takes the plant from Gilgamesh, preventing him from receiving the plant's benefits. Gilgamesh's friend, Enkidu, is created by the Sumerian god Aruru out of clay in the image of the god Anu.[9] Anu is the Sumerian god of the heavens.

- *The Enuma Elish*, a Babylonian myth from the early 2nd Millennium BCE. The first two lines are translated as, "When on high, before the heavens were named. Firm ground below had not been called by name." These lines have echoes in P's Genesis 1.1, *"In the beginning when God created the heavens and earth."* In the *Enuma Elish* the god Marduk kills Tiamat, the chaotic god of salt water, splits her in two, and creates the dome of the sky from half of her body and the earth from the other half. This resonates with P's creation of the waters above the dome of the sky and the waters in the earth. Since P may have written his creation story in Babylon during the exile, he would have been very familiar with the *Enuma Elish*, Babylon's creation story. In the text, man is created from the blood of a god defeated in the creation myth.[10] As in *Gilgamesh*, there is a hint of man's creation in the image of a god, a major theme in P's creation story.

---

9. Westermann, 37. Also, J. M. Sasson, "Gilgamesh Epic," ABD, vol 2, 1025f. And in Richard J. Clifford, *Creation Accounts in the Ancient Near East and in the Bible* (Washington, DC: The Catholic Biblical Quarterly Monograph Series 27: The Catholic Biblical Association of America: 1994), 6; he states that the creation of Enkidu, "was the contribution of the Akkadian composer; it was not in the Sumerian source."

10. W. G. Lambert, "Enuma Elish," ABD, Vol. 2, 528. Clay may also be inferred in the creation of man.

- *Atrahasis*, an early Akkadian myth, also from the early 2nd Millennium BCE, at least 750 years before the writing of Adam and Eve.[11] In *Atrahasis*, man is created from clay and the blood of a slain minor god, known as an Igigi, also hinting at man's creation in an image of a god, similar to the same hint in the *Enuma Elish*.

  The clay from which man was made in the Euphrates valley would have been as familiar to the Sumerians and their successors, the Akkadians, as the dust from which Adam was made was familiar to the Israelites living in their frequently arid land.

These stories constitute a creation genre. This will be even clearer later, when we analyze the flood story and see the close connection between the biblical account and virtually all of the Mesopotamian creation myths. There are many other Mesopotamian myths that have echoes in J's creation stories.

To clarify my use of the term "genre," here is an example of a genre from our own modern culture, the Western cinema and book, characterized by the following elements:

- The hero wears a white hat;
- the villain wears a black hat.
- The hero always wins in the end, and
- while he has dysfunctional relations with women,
- he has very close and functional relationships with horses.

Many Mesopotamian creation myths had similar patterns.

All of the Mesopotamian creation myths were written or copied in the cuneiform writing system, believed to have originated with the Sumerian language, and evolved to other languages, including Akkadian. The cuneiform wedges, "express phonetic syllables divorced from any semantic meaning."[12] similar to the way our alphabet is used in many

---

11. There is a copy by a known scribe in training named Nur-Aya, and dated c 1700 BCE. Clifford, 75.

12. Jerrold S. Cooper, "Cuneiform," ABD, Vol. 1, 1215.

modern languages. The Akkadian version of the cuneiform writing system was the exclusive diplomatic writing system used in the Ancient Near East (ANE) from about 1500 to 500 BCE. Most official correspondence from one country to another in the ANE during those 1000 years was written in Akkadian. The ANE composed the entire civilized world at that time with the possible exception of a part of the Indian peninsula. Although Greece began to recover from its dark age with the writings of Homer circa 800 or 700 BCE, Greek culture did not really flower until 200 or more years later.

Therefore, all scribes in the ANE, including Israelite scribes, had to learn the cuneiform writing system and the Akkadian language, and they learned it by copying *Gilgamesh*, *Enuma Elish*, *Atrahasis*, and countless other Mesopotamian writings over and over. J was almost certainly a scribe, since, in his time, it is likely that the vast majority of the population was illiterate, and many if not most literate people were scribes and knew Akkadian. J, then, would have been familiar with the Mesopotamian myths and their well-established genres.

Ancient authors tended to organize their writings around accepted genres but exercised great freedom inside the genre. Knowing that J's creation stories in Genesis often use well known genres helps us direct our attention away from the elements of the genres. We can then focus on the important new messages in the myths by noting the differences between J's creation myths and the earlier ones he used as a frame for his stories.

The trick, then, in reading the biblical creation stories is not to concentrate on the genre (e.g., the flood), but to concentrate on the differences inside the genre.[13] For example, suppose a friend is telling you about a Western movie she has just seen, and she says,

> "The hero wore a white hat and the villain a black hat. The hero won in the end, but he had problems relating with the female star, although he got along very well with his horse."

This account would not tell you anything except that it was a familiar genre, a Western. To distinguish this from other Westerns, she would

---

13. Those who look for the ark from the flood do not understand how the Bible was written, and, thus, fail to recognize the purpose of the flood story.

have to tell you other details about the plot and the characters, details that would set the movie apart from other Westerns.

Here are some examples of the vital differences that set the biblical creation stories apart from the Mesopotamian myths:

a. The earlier Mesopotamian myths had man created for the sole purpose of serving the gods, e.g., relieving them from backbreaking tasks like digging the channels for the Euphrates and the Tigris rivers. As an example, the god Marduk says in the *Enuma Elish*,

> "I will establish a savage, man shall be his name...He shall be charged with the service of the gods that they may be at ease"[14]

Also, in *Atrahasis*, the Goddess Mami says on the creation of humans to the gods:

> "I have removed your heavy load, your work I have imposed on a 'man.' You raised a complaint over 'man' status. I have loosed the yoke! Freedom have I established!"[15]

Note how different these are from P's account where "humankind" is to supervise creation, acting as a partner of God, not a slave.

b. *In Atrahasis*, the blood of the god conveys life; while in Genesis 2.7, "...the Lord God...breathed into (Adam's) nostrils the breath of life."[16] Note that creation in both the Genesis 1 and 2 myths is not caused by violence as it is in *Atrahasis* (for the

---

14. As quoted in Westermann, 36.

15. Old Babylonian version, supplemented by Late Babylonian and Assyrian recensions. Translation at Biblical Archaeological Society Seminar, St. Edmund Hall, Oxford University, August, 1999.

16. Also, Ezekiel. 37.5, "... to these (dry) bones: I will cause breath to enter you, and you shall live.

    creation of humanity) and *Enuma Elish* (where the god Marduk kills the god Tiamot to create the world).

c. In many Mesopotamian myths, man seems to be created immortal,[17] with the power to reproduce, a combination inevitably leading to a disastrous population explosion. Thus, the Mesopotamian gods did not excel in long range planning. While less than perfect long range planning is also a characteristic of J's God, in J's account, man is created mortal, not immortal (because God says, in Genesis 3.2, [Adam] "might reach out his hand and take also from the tree of life, and eat, and live forever").

d. There is precedent for the tree of life in Mesopotamian myths, but the tree of the knowledge of good and evil is original with J. It is thought to represent, "the superior spiritual-ethical religion which is characteristic of the school of J."[18]

These significant differences tell us what J and P and their generations thought of man, man's relationship with God, man's purpose, and how these concepts had advanced since the earlier Mesopotamian myths.

There are many misconceptions that have arisen from questionable interpretations and translations of some of the elements of these stories. Here is a story (no doubt an urban myth) told to me by an acquaintance from Atlanta.

> A freshman legislator from the bible belt rose to speak in favor of a proposed law to make English the official language of Georgia. After speaking for 10 minutes, he came to what he thought was a clinching argument. He said, "The Bible was written in English, and I think if it was good enough for Moses it ought to be good enough for Georgia."

The point of the story is to remind us that the Old Testament was not originally written in English, but in Hebrew, and translations can be tricky, as we shall now see.

---

17. In Atrahasis, man is explicitly immortal; Gilgamesh, although semi-divine, is not created immortal.

18. Westermann, 186–187.

What do the words "Adam" and "Eve" mean?

"Adam" is derived from the Hebrew word *adamah*, which means surface of the earth, or ground. The Hebrew term *adam*, means mankind or humanity, created from the *adamah*. There are 555 occurrences of *adam* in the Old Testament, usually in the form *ha adam*, the man, and it predominantly means humankind in Genesis 2 and 3.[19] As Claus Westermann writes, "Adam does not mean an individual, (not even as exemplar or archetype) but the species, humankind… The use of Adam in the New Testament, especially in Paul, with its distinctive meaning in the story of salvation, is not Old Testament usage."[20] But many scholars disagree and point out that, for example, Genesis 2.25 refers to *ha adam* and his *ishah* (woman). There are many other passages in Genesis 2 and 3 where *adam* refers to both mankind in general and to an individual, an indication of J's complexity and ambiguity.

In the New Revised Standard Version of the bible (NRSV), the words "humanity," "the man," and "Adam" are all translations of the Hebrew *ha adam*, and stand for mankind, humanity, our species, and, perhaps occasionally, the man, Adam. Further, when the term stands for mankind, *ha adam* is androgynous; i.e., Adam is both male and female. The Priestly writer, P, confirms this in Genesis 1.27, "So God created humankind in his image,…male and female he created them." While this translation does not specifically tell us that Adam was androgynous, when we know that "humankind" is a translation of *ha adam* (Adam), and could read, "So God created [*Adam*] in his image…male and female he created *them*," (emphasis mine) it is confirmed.

So, Adam is plural and both male and female. Therefore, Eve is a part of Adam before being separated/created. There is other support for this understanding in the text.

---

19. But, in Genesis 4.1, Adam and Eve seem to appear for the first time as persons, "Now the man (*ha adam*) knew his wife Eve and she conceived and bore Cain." This verse is the work of J, according to Campbell and O'Brien, 94. In Genesis 4.25, it is clearer that Adam is an individual because he is referred to without the definite article (<u>man</u>, not <u>the man</u>), "Adam (*adam* without the definite article *ha*) knew "his wife" [the Hebrew for "his wife" is *ishto*] again, and she bore a son, and named him Seth." See page 17 where Campbell and O'Brien assign 4.25 to an unknown source; but Westermann assigns 4.25 to J.

20. Westermann, p, 202.

- Eve told the serpent she knows of the prohibition not to eat the fruit from the tree of the knowledge of good and evil, even though God told it only to Adam. We are left believing either that Adam told her of this prohibition, which is not supported in the text, or that she knew it because she was part of Adam when God laid down the injunction, which does have support in the text.
- As our experience confirms, Eve (i.e., women) also will die and return to dust, even though God lays that punishment only on the androgynous *ha adam*.
- God expels *ha adam* from the garden (Genesis 3.24, "He drove out the man…"), but does not specifically expel Eve, even though we know Eve also left, because in the next chapter she conceives a child with Adam.

The most logical explanation for these omissions is that Eve was part of *ha adam* and did not need to be named.

This last observation adds additional support for the two source theory that suggests that Chapters 2 and 3 came from different sources. In Chapter 2, the female part of Adam is separated into "woman." But, in Chapter 3, the term Adam still seems to refer to both the male and female inhabitants of Eden; i.e., Adam still seems androgynous and plural. Eve in Hebrew is *havah*, and the term means "one who gives life." Eve does not receive her name until after the punishment of the man and woman in Chapter 3 (with the first J reference to reproduction). Until then she is always "woman." (*ishah*). She is also referred to as "his wife" (*ishto*). Her name, Eve, is clearly a generality for women, although she also seems to act as an individual in some of her dealings with Adam.[21]

There is an interesting side to the translation of Adam's rib. Almost all translations I am aware of has Eve made from Adam's rib.[22] The Hebrew word translated as rib (*tsaylah*) occurs many times in the Bible, and

---

21. And Eve seems to be named as a person in Chapter 4. See footnote 19 above.

22. An exception to the rib translation was that of the great Jewish scholar, Rabbi Shlomo Yitzhaki (Solomon, son of Isaac), of Troyes (1040-1105 CE), known as Rashi, who translated it as "side."

is predominantly translated as side, not rib.[23] According to J. B. Prichard, the rib translation predominates due to the common love of word play in the ANE. In the Sumerian language, there is a connection between the words for "rib" and "the lady who makes life," which is a good translation for the Hebrew name for Eve.[24] But only a few scholars are aware of this word play and its significance has been lost on the vast majority of Bible readers for many centuries. Further, this translation diminishes Eve's origin (*ha adam* being split gives a woman more status than if she is made from a rib). Future translators should consider a change to side. Rib may be yet another example of tradition trumping rationality.

For another interesting dispute on translating Hebrew to English, see Appendix I.

Did sin enter the world through Eve's action?

Many Christians would say yes. But, neither P nor J—nor any of the other authors of the Hebrew Bible—specifically blame Eve. For example, J writes in Genesis 6.5,

> "When Yahweh saw that the wickedness of *(ha adam)* was great on earth, and every planning and striving of its heart was always wicked, he was sorry that he had made *(ha adam)* on earth, and he was grieved at heart."

And in Genesis 8.21, J has God say,

> "...for the inclination of the human *(ha adam)* heart is evil from youth."

---

23. Francis Brown, S.R. Driver, and Charles A. Briggs, *The Brown-Driver-Briggs Hebrew and English Lexicon* (Houghton, Mifflin and Company: Boston: 1906) 854, concordance number 6,763. For example, *tsaylah* is frequently used to describe the side of a hill, a temple, or of the tabernacle.

24. J.B. Pritchard, *Man's Predicament in Eden:* 1948–1949, 5, "...in Sumerian there is established through a play upon words, a definite connection between the rib and 'the lady who makes life.'" As quoted in Westermann, 230.

There is no mention of Eve's sole role in this wickedness in either quote. In fact, there is no reference in the Hebrew Bible, and none in the Protestant Old Testament supporting any idea of Eve's guilt. In the Hebrew Bible, sin enters the world because, in the hearts of man, there is *yetser ha ra*, Hebrew for "evil inclination;" and there is no specific connection between *yetser ha ra* and Eve in J or any other part of the Hebrew Bible or Protestant Old Testament.

The first mention of Eve as the one responsible for sin is in the book of *Ecclesiasticus*, Chapter 25, verse 24, "From a woman sin had its beginning, and because of her we all die." Ecclesiasticus, also known as the Wisdom of Ben Sirach, was written about 200 BCE, between 350 and 750 years after J's writings (depending on whose dating of J you accept). This book is not included in the Hebrew or Protestant Bible, although it is included in Roman Catholic and more orthodox Bibles and in the Protestant Apocrypha.

Ecclesiasticus was written during the period of great Hellenistic influence on Jewish writers, and it is quite possible that Ben Sirach was influenced by the story of Pandora's box, the Greek myth blaming the start of the world's problems on women.

If Eve is not responsible for evil, did J's God create evil?

Most of us believe that man was created with free will. If our only choice is the good, do we really have free will? How can we, in the absence of the possibility of evil, really have free will? God probably left open the possibility we would choose evil.

I believe that J took Gilgamesh's thieving serpent, and, with great narrative and theological skill, turned the serpent into a symbol of temptation. Eve responded to the serpent in a very human way—she was curious, interested, and thirsting for knowledge.

This is a good example of the timelessness of mythological truth as it describes common human characteristics.

Concerning the word translated as helper, in Genesis 2.18, we read,

> "Then the Lord God said, 'it is not good that man should be alone, I will make him a helper as his partner."

The Hebrew word translated as helper is *ezer*. Helper is too weak to be a good translation. It even suggests subservience. Robert Alter translates it as "sustainer," and Rashi, as "counterpart;" both of these choices imply a more equal relationship. *The New Oxford Annotated Bible* (NRSV) notes on page 4 that, "Helper (is) not in a relationship of subordination but of mutuality and interdependence."

Psalm 121.2 states, "My help comes from the Lord, who made heaven and earth." God is a helper (*ezer*) to Israel. And God's relationship to Israel is hardly weak or subservient.

As to the punishment God inflicts on "the woman" [*ha isha*, not *havah (Eve)*],

> "To the woman he said, 'I will greatly increase your pangs in childbearing; in pain you shall bring forth children, yet your desire shall be for your husband, and he shall rule over you." (Genesis 3.16)

Was J trying to explain why women had so much difficulty in childbirth compared to the sheep and goats that seemed to give birth with little or no trouble? If so, the irony is that J was right. Women do have more difficulty in childbirth because man has achieved knowledge, whether from the tree or elsewhere. Evolutionary scientists believe that the human skull expanded over the last two million years, while women's childbearing anatomy did not expand in pace.[25] Thus, the "knowledge" acquired by mankind over eons has resulted in women's greater "pain" in childbirth.

As to the statement that husbands "will rule over" wives, that is an accurate description of the patriarchal system that pertained for thousands of years until recent decades.

As to the punishment God inflicts on the man, in Genesis 3.17 we read:

---

25. In the September, 2003 issue of *Discover* magazine, page 37, Carl Zimmer writes, "Our brains are not just big—they are grotesquely huge. A typical mammal our size would have a brain one-seventh a large as ours... From 7 million to 2 million years ago, our ancestors had brains about the size of a modern chimpanzee's. Hominid brains...began to increase 2 million years ago, and they continued to balloon...until they neared their present size at least 160,000 years ago."

"Because you have listened to your wife, and have eaten of the tree about which I commanded you 'you shall not eat of it,' cursed is the ground because of you; in toil you shall eat of it all the days of your life; in thorns and thistles it shall bring forth for you; and you shall eat the plants of the field. By the sweat of your face you shall eat bread until you return to the ground, for out of it you were taken, you are dust, and to dust you shall return."

Man's punishment confirms the overwhelmingly agricultural economy in ancient Israel. Man had to work hard in order to achieve sufficient food. And man was subject to problems not under his control: weeds, drought, plagues, pests, blight, floods, etc. Most of us, and remember *ha adam* refers to both men and women, have had to work hard to support ourselves and our families; and our success, economic or otherwise, has been in spite of obstacles outside of our control.

These passages, among other things, are etiologies; explanations of causes, right or wrong. They purport to tell us why life was so hard for Israelites in J's day. It is interesting to note how little has changed in 3,000 years.

Why were Adam and Eve expelled from Eden?

Is it because they disobeyed the Lord?

Note that God curses the serpent and the ground but does not curse either Adam or Eve after they eat the fruit of the Tree of the Knowledge of Good and Evil. Further, note that immediately after God metes out his punishment, in Genesis 3.21,

> "the Lord God made garments of skins for… man [*adam*, not *ha adam*] and for his wife *[ishto]*, and clothed them."

Like an angry parent, God continues to care for his disobedient children. Then in Genesis 3.22, 23,

> "the Lord God said, 'See, the man has become like one of us, knowing good and evil; and now, he might reach out his hand and take also

from the tree of life, and eat, and live forever'—*therefore* the Lord God sent him forth from the garden of Eden..." [emphasis mine]

Note how the concern that man may become immortal impels God to action. And note the Lord's concern about *ha adam* becoming "like one of us," a clearly plural construction. The question is, which "us" did J mean? It is probable that J meant one of God's council, but not the Lord *(YHWH)*. The inference of God's council is also in Genesis 1.26, "Let *us* make humankind in our image" (emphasis mine). It is also explicit in Job 1.6, "One day, the heavenly beings[26] came to present themselves before the Lord." There are other plural examples.

God had created man distinctly separate from the god-like divine creatures, the animals, and all other creation. Man is to exist as a separate being. Other verses in Genesis suggest that J's God seems very serious about this distinct separation in his creation. If Adam becomes even more like a god, he will not be the man he was created to be.[27]

Here are the critical questions:

- Was Eve's eating of the fruit a good or bad act on her part?
- Was Adam's expulsion from Eden a good or bad result?
- Should we want to return to Eden?

Traditionally, the expulsion has been considered an unmitigated tragedy. But note Genesis 2.25, before Eve's encounter with the serpent,

"And the man and his wife were both naked, and were not ashamed."

Who or what do we know that is, "naked and...not ashamed?" I suggest, in general, only animals and young children are naked and unashamed.

---

26. In both Job 1.6 and 2.1 "the heavenly beings" are a translation from the Hebrew, "the sons of *Elohim*" or, "the sons of God."

27. The confusing passages, Chapter 6: 1-4 hint that the mating of "sons of God" and daughters of men was displeasing to God; and one may assume it was because of God's desire to keep man separate from gods. Also, the Tower of Babel story in Genesis 11 may illustrate God's displeasure at man's attempt to be more than God intends.

And, in Genesis 3.5, the Serpent says,

"for God knows that when you eat of it your eyes will be opened, and you will be like God (the Jewish Publication Society Bible has divine beings), knowing good and evil."

If the fruit was not eaten, would our eyes have remained closed. Would we remain like animals or children, not knowing the difference between "good and evil?" Would we prefer a life of unknowing, or would we prefer to face the daily choices of good or evil paths? It is possible that, typical of the many complexities of life, there is a good and bad side of Eve's transgression. She did disobey God, certainly a dangerous and questionable act. But, on the other hand, do we want to return to Eden, and be "naked and…not ashamed"—unknowing? Do we want to lose "the knowledge of good and evil," generally taken to mean all knowledge? J, as usual, revels in this kind of complexity. J's Genesis 2-3 may be a myth about man's growing up, becoming an adult.

Here are some other examples of J's ambiguity in his Adam and Eve story:

- Men and women *(Ha adam)* must work hard, but they do get food.
- Women *(ishah)* have difficult labors, but do give life.
- In Genesis Chapters 2 and 3 man *(ha adam)* is told to eat only plants, thus sparing animals the concern they might become food. But, in 3.21, God specifically uses animal skins to clothe Adam and Eve during the time man is not to harm animals. How can we understand this seeming contradiction? How does God get the skins from animals without harming them? Does he wait until they die a natural death? Later, in 9.2f, God gives animals to Noah as approved food. Does the oral tradition behind 3.21 come after the oral tradition behind 9.2f?
- There is ongoing confusion between "the man" *(ha adam)*, "man" *(ish)*, "Eve" *(havah)*, "woman" *(ishah)*, and "his wife" *(ishto)*. For example, when God is meting out punishment, "the woman" is

ishah, not *havah* (Eve), but the man is *ha adam* (mankind), not *ish* (man); thus implying that "the man's" punishment applies to mankind which includes women *(ishah)*.

- After "woman" is split from the androgynous Adam, Adam seems to continue to be androgynous and plural.
- Later, in the Tower of Babel story in Chapter 11, we find that God disapproves of the building of the Tower and causes dispersion. But this dispersion populates the earth, which is one of God's commands to both P and J (see P's Genesis 9.7, "abound on the earth and multiply in it." And J's Genesis 9.19, "These three were the sons of Noah; and from these the whole earth was peopled.").

Genesis Chapter 4 begins in the NRSV with the words, "Now when the man knew his wife Eve, and she conceived," that sounds like "the man," which we know is *ha adam*, and "his wife Eve" (*havah ishto*) are real people and not symbols of our species as a whole, as they are throughout almost all of Chapters 2 and 3.

Scholars agree that Chapter 4, verses 1 through 16 (and probably 17–24) were written by J, because his fingerprints are quite evident there. God is referred to as Lord *(YHWH)* ten times,[28] and *YHWH* meets with, and talks to, Cain, a characteristic of J.

An alternate interpretation would have Adam and Eve still representing our species and not individuals; "Now when the man knew his wife Eve, and she conceived," would then be a description of how human reproduction began. If this is right, the mystery then shifts to Cain and Abel. Are they individuals or just representatives of farmers and shepherds?

Cain was a farmer and Abel, a shepherd; some scholars have made a point of seeing their conflict as general hostility between those two occupations, perhaps like the range wars between farmers and ranchers in Wyoming and elsewhere in our West in the late 19th century. As enticing as that interpretation is, there is no direct support in the text. Westermann says, "The conflict does not arise from the difference between the occupations and the narrative does not set them in

---

28. Verses 1, 3, 4, 6, 9, 10, 13, 15 (twice), and 16.

opposition. The conflict arises from the acceptance and nonacceptance of the offerings of the produce… This means then that the real critical area of the narrative does not lie in the conflict of occupations, but…in God's decision in favor of Abel and against Cain manifest in the acceptance and nonacceptance of the offerings. The consequence of the decision is the 'darkening' of Cain's countenance which leads to the murder of his brother."[29]

Also important is that after Cain kills Abel and is found out by God, Cain worries that his status as a fugitive and wanderer will cause others to kill him. J's God then tells Cain in verse 15,

> " 'Whoever kills Cain will suffer a seven-fold vengeance.' And the Lord put a mark on Cain, so that no one who came upon him would kill him."

While one may wonder what a seven-fold vengeance would be, and the nature of the mark God put on Cain, I think the important question is why did God protect Cain from other men after he murdered his brother?

After all, in Chapter 9, verse 6, P's God tells Noah,

> "Whoever sheds the blood of a human, by a human shall that person's blood be shed."

Perhaps the explanation is that since P's Chapter 9 is after J's Chapter 4 in Genesis—and P wrote later than J—in Cain's world, there is no law. The only law God had laid down prior to the Cain and Abel story is that the fruit of the Tree of the Knowledge of Good and Evil may not be eaten. Since Cain has never been in the Garden of Eden, nor can he ever go there, there are no laws for him to obey. So, by killing Abel, Cain did not disobey an extant specific law of God. J's God, in effect, was operating by the seat of his pants, and continued to do so until P's bare bones covenant given to Noah in Chapter 9, after the flood. In any event, J frequently leaves gaps in his narrative and does not explain actions in detail. Tikva Frymer-Kensky, a Professor in the Divinity School at the University of Chicago, stated in a lecture in Spring, 2001, that she believes this is purposeful on J's part in order to leave room for different interpretations of the text.

---

29. Westermann, 294.

The last two verses of Genesis, Chapter 4 (25 and 26), may be part of the genealogical material so characteristic of P.[30]

The Flood

The flood myth has its sources in Mesopotamian myths. We heard earlier about three of them. Here, I will substitute the *Sumerian Flood Story* for the *Enuma Elish* which does not include a flood story:

The Gilgamesh Epic, a myth written in Akkadian with Sumerian sources, originated before 2000 BCE. One version, with references to a flood but without a flood story, dates from c. 1800 BCE. Other versions include a flood story and are later. As we learned earlier, *Gilgamesh* includes a plant that rejuvenates life (but not a plant of the Knowledge of Good and Evil), and a serpent that takes the plant from Gilgamesh. The later *Gilgamesh* also includes:

- a flood with a sole survivor/hero named Utnapishtim, and
- Utnapishtim's release of (in this order) a dove, a swallow, and a raven (while Noah's order is a raven, a dove and a dove), and
- Utnapishtim's immortality after the flood, and
- Gilgamesh's failure to attain immortality.

The Sumerian Flood Story is dated no earlier than perhaps 1750 BCE, "the Late Old Babylonian period."[31] In this Sumerian myth, creation emanates from Enki. There is a trinity of gods at the top of all the other gods: Anu is the god of the heavens, Enlil is the god of the earth, and Enki is the god under the earth.[32] In this flood story, "Enlil took a dislike to mankind because the clamor of their shouting...kept him sleepless."[33]

---

30. Campbell and O'Brien 95, note 4.

31. Clifford, Richard J., *Creation Accounts in the Ancient Near East and in the Bible* (Washington, DC: The Catholic Biblical Quarterly Monograph Series 27, The Catholic Biblical Association of America: 1994), 42.

32. Ibid., 52. Clifford states that Enki, the personification of underground spring water, the source of rivers and waters that fertilized the earth, was the creator, because he is the god of fertility (causing the blooming of the earth) and wisdom (causing the advent of culture).

33. Ibid., 43.

The gods, then, decided to send a flood to kill all humans. But Enki secretly warned the pious king Ziusudra. At this point, there is a break in the tablets, but we assume Enki told Ziusudra to build a boat, because, when the surviving text continues, it describes the flood, after which Ziusudra emerges from the boat to offer a sacrifice.

After another break, we find Ziusudra prostrate before Enlil and Anu who confer eternal life on Ziusudra. And so, in the *Sumerian Flood Story*, there is,

- a flood with a sole survivor/hero named Ziusudra.
- and, while man becomes mortal after the flood, the hero, King Ziusudra becomes immortal.

Atrahasis, means "very wise" in Akkadian. At least five older traditions are incorporated in the *Atrahasis* myth. The rebellion of the minor gods, called Igigi, and the formation of man as substitute workers draws on the Sumerian Epic, *Enki and Ninmah*. The flood tradition is patterned on four earlier Sumerian Epics: the just-introduced *Sumerian Flood Story*, some versions of the *Sumerian King List*, the standard version of *Gilgamesh XI*, and the *Rulers of Lagash*.[34] This is a good example of how ancient authors, like J, relied on extant creation genres in producing their stories.

The myth of *Atrahasis* begins with the lesser gods, the Igigi, doing the backbreaking work for the senior gods, the Anunnaki. After many years, the Igigi refused to continue, and Enki and the mother goddess, Mami, both senior gods, solved the problem by creating human workers from clay and the flesh and blood of an Igigi god, probably the leader of the rebellion. After 600 years, humans increased in overwhelming numbers. Enlil and his fellow senior gods decided to destroy the human race by a series of plagues, culminating in a world-wide flood. Atrahasis and his family survived, but only because Atrahasis was warned and counseled by the god Enki to build an ark. The gods, deprived of their human servants, realized how dependent on their human workers they had become. Therefore they relented and allowed re-population while

---

34. Ibid. 75–76.

adding safeguards against overpopulation in the form of mortality and limits of reproduction.[35]

Atrahasis in particular creates a model for J to follow in Genesis. In Atrahasis there is,

- A flood with a sole survivor/hero named Atrahasis.
- A warning from a god (Enki) that the flood is coming.
- The recommendation to build a boat.
- The death of the rest of humanity.
- The making of a sacrifice to the gods after the flood subsides.
- The enduring mortality of the hero, Atrahasis (like Noah).
- There is a solution to overpopulation; i.e., more women are infertile, virginity is required in women dedicated to a deity, and more children die.

The Genesis flood story has significant parallels to these episodes in *Atrahasis*.

There is an interesting contradiction in the Genesis flood story. In 6.7, J has the Lord state,

"I will blot out from the earth the human beings I have created."
And, in 6.13 P has God tell Noah,

"I have determined to make an end of all flesh, for the earth is full of violence because of them."

After determining to end all humankind, God then instructs Noah to build an ark so he and his family will survive, a clear contradiction to his intentions just quoted. How can we understand this? It becomes clearer when we recall the dispute between the god Enlil, who wants to destroy all humans, and the god Enki, who wants to save a remnant

---

35. Ibid., 74–75. Some translations read "1,200 years" rather than "600 years." For example, see *Atrahasis* quotation on page 60.

family for re-population. Obviously, J and P are stuck with only one God, and they do the best they can with the tension in the story created by that limitation. But this contradiction and tension is further confirmation of the use of the Mesopotamian flood story genre by P and J.[36]

In many of these earlier flood stories, it seems that the gods decided to destroy man because man was created immortal and with the ability to reproduce (a clear mistake by the gods). Therefore, overpopulation was an inevitable problem, and the gods could not sleep because man made so much noise. For example, in *Atrahasis* we read:

> "Twelve hundred years had not passed. The land extended. The people multiplied. The land became as loud as a wild ox. At their noise the god was disturbed; Enlil heard their racket. He addressed the great gods: 'The racket of 'mankind' is too burdensome. By their noise I am deprived of sleep.'"[37]

In Genesis 6.5, J wrote that God destroyed man because he had become evil, not because he was loud. In Genesis, man was punished because of his social behavior, not because of noise caused by over population. Bad (perhaps even sinful) behavior does not seem to be noticed in the Mesopotamian creation myths. Here is J's statement in Genesis 6.5,

> "The Lord saw that the wickedness of humankind was great in the earth, and that every inclination of the thoughts of their hearts was only evil continually."[38]

This may be the first time in the ANE creation myths that human moral behavior caused a god to consider eliminating mankind. Earlier ANE writings (e.g., the 18th century BCE Code of Hammurapi), do include human moral behavior as a concern of the gods; but these writings

---

36. Ronald S. Hendel, "Genesis, Book of," ABD, Vol. 2, 939.

37. Old Babylonian version, supplemented by the Late Babylonian and Assyrian recensions and translated for the Biblical Archeological Society Seminar, St. Edmund Hall, Oxford University, August, 1999.

38. Campbell and O'Brien attribute this passage to J, 95.

are not sacred myths but legal literature, and they primarily relate to the King's concern with effective government.

The opening four verses of Genesis, Chapter 6, seem to be a fragment from a very old oral tradition that the ultimate editors (technically, the redactors) decided to insert here, possibly because they could not find a more logical fit elsewhere. It does not seem to be connected to the flood story, and it is certainly not attributable to either P or J. Here is what these mysterious verses say:

> "When people began to multiply on the face of the ground, and daughters were born to them, the sons of God saw that they were fair; and they took wives for themselves of all that they chose. Then the Lord said, 'My spirit shall not abide in mortals forever, for they are flesh; their days shall be one hundred twenty years.' The Nephilim were on the earth in those days—and also afterward—when the sons of God went into the daughters of humans, who bore children to them. These were the heroes that were of old, warriors of renown."

These verses raise at least three questions:

1. Where did these "sons of God" come from? We have heard nothing about them earlier in Genesis. A Dutch scholar, Ellen van Wolde, pointed out that this could not refer to angels because angels are a product of a much later historical period. She wrote, "speaking of the sons of god as angels [in this passage] would be like…having Solomon walk around in an Armani suit."[39]

In Psalm 89.6–7 we read,

> "Who among the heavenly beings[40] is like the Lord, a God feared in the council of the holy ones, great and awesome above all that are around him?"

---

39. Ellen van Wolde, *Stories of the Beginning* (Morehouse Publishing: 1995), 112.
40. The Hebrew, translates as "sons of elim," which is probably taken from the Canaanite "sons of ilm" meaning, "sons of El," suggesting Canaanite echoes in this Psalm.

And in Job 1.6 and 2.1,

> "One day the heavenly beings [the Hebrew is, "sons of Elohim" (God)] came to present themselves before the Lord."

The sons of God, then, belong to a class of heavenly beings or gods.

2. What is the meaning of this limit of 120 years? Is it meant as a maximum life span after the flood? Perhaps not, even though it is probable that the oral tradition behind Genesis 6.1-4 predated J's flood story. P tells us that Arpachshad, not an antediluvian figure, since he was born two years after the flood, lived 438 years.[41] This alleged maximum seems later to emerge as an optimum since Moses died at age 120.[42]

3. And who are the Nephilim? And, "the heroes that were of old, warriors of renown?" Both, apparently, are very old traditions, but no hard evidence helps us identify them.

As mysterious and confusing as these verses are, here again we find the hint of God's displeasure of the mixing of divines and humans, a confirmation of his displeasure at Adam's effort to attain divine attributes—and as God says, "be like one of us."

There are several conflicting passages from the J and P account of the flood. Here is one of them. J writes, in Genesis 7.2:

> "Take with you seven pairs of all clean animals…and a pair of the animals that are not clean…"

J has God call for seven pairs of clean animals, but only one pair of unclean animals, because he is concerned about having enough clean animals for sacrifices.

P writes, in Genesis 6.19:

---

41. Genesis 11.10–12.
42. Deuteronomy 34.7.

"And of every living thing, of all flesh, you shall bring two of every kind into the ark…"

P has God call for only one pair of all animals. He sees no need for sacrificial animals following the flood since it precedes the exodus where, P believes, acceptable sacrifice is introduced for the first time. Thus, one pair of each animal is enough. In contrast, note that before the flood and before the exodus, J has Cain and Abel make offerings in Genesis 4.3,4; Abel's offering being a lamb.

In J's Genesis 8.20, Noah made a sacrifice to God in thanks for his family's survival of the flood. This was a common way to show gratitude in the ANE (e. g., Ziusudra in the *Sumerian Flood Story* and Atrahasis in *Atrahasis*, precedents ignored by P).

We can easily see that Genesis 8.20f is the work of J,

"Then Noah built an altar to the Lord, and took of every clean animal and of every clean bird, and offered burnt offerings on the altar… the Lord smelled the pleasing odor."

There are three clues here as to the author:

1. the reference to "the Lord" *(YHWH)* before Moses receives the name in Exodus, a sign of J;
2. an odor pleasing to the Lord, indicating J's non-transcendental *YHWH*, and
3. a sacrifice before P's sanction of sacrifice in Exodus,[43] also a sign of J. While, as noted, there were sacrifices in the ANE before the exodus, this is still an indication of J since P does not report any sacrifices before Exodus.

In *Atrahasis*, man explicitly loses his immortality and becomes mortal after the flood. The same result may be inferred in *Gilgamesh* and other Mesopotamian myths. J cannot follow that part of the genre in Genesis because man is already mortal, but there is an echo of the

---

43. P writes instructions for the construction of the Altar in Exodus 27 and instructions for offerings in Exodus 29.

older myths here. Before the flood, the record life span, according to P, was held by Methuselah, who lived 969 years. After the flood, man's life span lessens.

In Genesis 1.29, P has God tell Adam,

> "I hand over to you every seed-bearing plant over the whole face of the earth and every tree with seed-bearing fruit; they are to serve you for food."

In Genesis 3.18, J has God tell Adam, "you shall eat the plants of the field." Initially, then, "the Man" (*ha adam*) was a vegetarian.

Finally, in Gen. 9.3f, after the flood, P begins God's covenant with Noah with a change in these vegetarian requirements by having God say, "Every creature that lives shall be yours to eat; as with the green grasses, I give you all these."[44]

P's Noah covenant continues with these commands:

> "you shall not eat flesh with its life, that is, its blood…Whoever sheds the blood of a human, by a human shall that person's blood be shed; for in his own image, God made humankind. And you, be fruitful and multiply, abound on the earth and multiply in it."

Note that this is not a covenant for Jews alone. It applies to everyone since, in Genesis, Noah's family was the sole survivor of the flood, and his sons were responsible for the re-population of the entire world.

This covenant at the end of the flood suggests that the wickedness that caused the flood might have been the murder of fellow men and the mistreatment of animals.

In Genesis 10, J tells us that Noah's three sons, Shem, Japheth, and Ham, will re-populate the whole earth. Ham had seen his drunken father naked, which in that culture, was a cause of great shame. And Noah curses, not Ham, but, surprisingly, his son Canaan. Since the main target of Israelite hatred in the 10th century BCE was Canaan, J takes this opportunity to create context and support for the enmity between these

---

44. The dietary laws that came later in Leviticus 11 limit the "creatures that you may eat."

two entities. The appropriately named son of Ham takes on the curse and shame of his father's act. And Israel's dislike of its enemy Canaan is both explained and reinforced.

P then tells us which son is the eponymous ancestor of which people.[45] Most of the names listed are not familiar, but here are the peoples they represent:

- Shem is the ancestor of the Israelites.
- Ham, through his cursed son Canaan, is the ancestor of Canaan itself, Cush (an early name for the Sudan), Ethiopia, Egypt, and (by extension) all of Africa, Babylonia, Assyria, Akkad, the Philistines, and probably (by extension) all of Asia.
- Japheth is ancestor of the Greeks[46] and the other peoples of the eastern Mediterranean, and (by extension) the future inhabitants of Europe, and (by further extension) North and South Americans of European descent.

Until at least 1500 CE, Europeans believed they were descendents of Japheth and entitled to the inheritance in Genesis 9.27, "May God make space for Japheth and let him live in the tents of Shem, and let Canaan be his slave." Being allowed to dwell in the tents of Shem, the ancestor of the Israelites, was a distinct honor to P.[47]

Canaan's diminished status as "slave" has caused much evil and sorrow in the world. This short verse of scripture has been ill-used over and over throughout history, at best to deem Africans inferior as alleged descendants of Canaan, and at worst to justify slavery.

Through the Middle Ages, almost all Christians and Jews believed in the literal truth of the Bible, including the assertion that Noah's sons were the source of all peoples of the then known world.[48]

---

45. An eponym is a place or a people whose name is taken from a person.

46. von Wolde, p 151f. Also, Victor P. Hamilton, *The Book of Genesis Chapters 1-17* (William B. Eerdmans Publishing Company: Grand Rapids) p.330f.

47. Was this verse added during the Hellenistic period after Alexander conquered the ANE? There seems to be no reason to provide this honor for the Greeks before the 3rd century BCE.

48. Also, see Acts 17.26, "From one ancestor he made all nations to inhabit the whole earth."

But, there is no provision in Genesis 10 for the re-population of the rest of the world. When Columbus stumbled on the New World, it raised the question, "where did the inhabitants of the New World fit into Noah's genealogy?"[49] This question resulted in doubt among many for the first time about the literal truth of the Bible. This doubt was instrumental in beginning the critical study of the Bible. Biblical research had its infantile start and then expanded rapidly almost one hundred years later after the 1690 publication of John Locke's book, *Essay Concerning Human Understanding*, generally considered the book most responsible for precipitating the Age of Enlightenment.

The Tower of Babel

J is the author of the brief Tower of Babel story in Genesis Chapter 11, verses 1-9. Scholars believe the name Babel is a late addition to the story and refers to Babylon, and the tower could refer to any of the large buildings known to have existed there. But the story is not about buildings; it is an etiology describing how languages and peoples became dispersed.

The Sumerians had a similar story about confusion of languages.[50] Ancient peoples in general thought there was only one language, because they never left their local habitat. Discovering other languages was puzzling and demanded an explanation. The Tower of Babel is one such explanation. There are similar stories explaining dispersion of peoples from many ancient cultures, many, like Noah's sons, with a connection to a flood story rather than a tower.[51]

Many scholars think the Tower of Babel story is the result of a long period of reworking much older oral traditions; these traditions may have dated back to the third millennium BCE or even earlier; they clearly predate any one of the several large Babylonian buildings referred to in the story, which were built in the late 2nd and early 1st millenniums BCE. Earlier oral

---

49. The tablets allegedly found by Joseph Smith, founder of the Church of Latter Day Saints, solved the problem by claiming that Shem's descendants migrated to the Americas in the pre-Christian era and possibly populated all of the Western Hemisphere.
50. The epic of Enmerkar, c 2000 BCE. Westermann, 539.
51. Westermann, 537-8.

and written traditions would have no reason to refer to Babylon.

God, in Genesis 11.6, is upset about the people of Babel.

> "'Look, they are one people; and they have all one language; and this is only the beginning of what they will do; nothing that they propose to do will now be impossible for them. Come, let us go down, and confuse their language there, so that they will not understand one another's speech.' So the Lord scattered them abroad from over the face of all the earth, and they left off building the city."

Once again, we have the threat of man being more than God wants him to be. So, God acts to keep man, so to speak, in his place. But, as previously noted, he also has made it known that he wants the earth filled with people. (P's God says to Noah, "Be fruitful and multiply, and fill the earth."[52] And J writes that "the sons of Noah will people the whole earth."[53])

God created man in the image of God, and reminds man of his identification with God in the Noah Covenant. But, in seeming contradiction, God does not want man to be too much like God (or, a god). A well-known scholar, Jeffrey Tigay, has reviewed the traditional view that man's creation in the image of God relates to common physical appearance. Tigay points out that Assyrian, Babylonian, and Egyptian cultures, so influential in the development of Israelite thought, used the concept of God's image metaphorically. He then states that the biblical reference may also be metaphorical, referring to common qualities, such as authority and judicial responsibility, rather than physical appearance. Tigay suggests that man is created with power over nature and has responsibility for justice—powers and responsibilities of a lower quality than God's, but similar to those of God. These are powers and responsibilities not shared by animals.[54] But these powers seem to make man into a creature, in God's terms, "like one of us."[55]

---

52. Genesis 9.1.

53. Genesis 9.19.

54. Jeffrey H. Tigay "The Image of God and the Flood: Some New Developments," *Studies in Jewish Education and Judaica in Honor of Louis Newman*, (New York: KTAV Publishing House: 1984).

55. Genesis 1.26; 9.6.

Final Comment on P's Creation Account in Genesis 1-2.4b.

To put P's creation account in perspective, the seven days of creation story may have been composed in Babylon by P in the mid to late 6th century, BCE. The Israelites were in exile in Babylon for forty-nine years from 587 to 538 BCE. They had been torn from their homes, wondering whether God would ever forgive them and let them return to Jerusalem. The only creation story they had was J's story in which Adam and Eve were exiled and sent East from Eden, just as the Israelites were sent East from Jerusalem to Babylon. As with God's judgment on Adam, the Israelites feared they would never be allowed to return to their homes. And they were powerless to create the opportunity for return. P's new creation story gave power to man. P writes in Genesis 1.28, "God blessed them,…and [gave them] dominion…over every living thing that moves on the earth." Their God also said His creation was "very good." (1.31). P's account suggests that God would forgive his people, giving them a morale boost and providing hope for a better future.

In all the creation myths in Mesopotamia and Israel that include floods, the genre follows the same order:

1. God (or gods) create man.
2. Man angers God (or gods).
3. God (or gods) destroys man, with the exception of one favored man (and his family).
4. God (or gods) relents, and allows the man's family to re-populate the earth, but with new limitations.

Again, we should not focus on the elements of the genre. The genre has interest as primordial history, that is, history of creation outside of time; but it is not history as we now know it. We should instead focus on the meaning imparted to us through the myth.

Conclusion

What important meanings are contained in the myths of Genesis 1-11?

The meanings are conveyed to us, in part by the changes from the prior Mesopotamian myths and, in part, by new elements not contained in the Mesopotamian myths. I believe the Biblical myths give us four important positive messages:

1. God's creation is "very good," and his creation includes us, *ha adam*.
2. God has created *ha adam* to be a partner, not a slave, in managing the earth—a big leap forward in self understanding and a big improvement in self esteem.
3. God is concerned about man's treatment of his fellow man and of animals; i.e., God is not only interested in ritual; he is also concerned with behavior—a big leap forward in our understanding of our responsibilities.

These three messages have endured and developed in Western civilization.

There is a fourth positive message. Different ideas about the nature of God are acceptable. This vital lesson may carry over from the polytheistic world which, in general, tolerated gods other than their own. Since P and J express different ideas about the nature of God, and their views are sanctioned in our Bible, we should be slow to condemn those whose ideas about God differ from our own. Thus, religious tolerance has some traction here. We will return to a more negative biblical message about religious tolerance in Chapter 5.

The single negative message in the biblical creation story is the curse of Canaan, which (perhaps unintentionally to the biblical author) has resulted in support for slavery and discrimination against people of African descent.

Appendix I

Comments on the Translation of the opening two Hebrew words in Genesis

Hebrew is read from right to left. A relatively minor issue that illustrates translation problems concerns the two opening Hebrew words in Genesis as translated into English in the New Revised Standard Version and the King James version:

"In the beginning when God created the heavens and the earth…"

The first word (pronounced: be-ray-SHEET) is a noun in construct, "the beginning of" something; it should be followed by a noun. Instead, it is followed by a verb (Pronounced: bah-RAH), "he created." The text literally reads "At the beginning of—he created." Since Hebrew has no vowels, the 11th century CE scholar Rashi felt justified in changing bah-RAH' to be-ROE, allowing the first two words to mean, "at the beginning of God's creation."[56] Hebrew is a complex ancient language, structured differently from Western languages, and be-rah SHEET bah-RAH (or be-ROE) can be translated many ways. The Living Bible, Robert Alter's translation, and the Jewish Publication Society Bible translate it as,

"When God began to create heaven and earth."

Why do they differ, and who is right? Here are the arguments for the translation, "When God began…"

"In the beginning" suggests that this was the beginning before which there was nothing. But the text itself suggests otherwise. The NRSV itself goes on to say that, "darkness covered the face of the deep, while a wind from God swept over the face of the waters."

So clearly there was, "the deep," and there was, "the face of the waters," before the beginning of Genesis 1. Translating be-rah-SHEET,

---

56. Tikva Frymer-Kensky, "Unwrapping the Torah," *Bible Review*, vol. XVIII, No. 5, Oct, 2002, 60.

"When God began to create heaven and earth," leaves open the possibility of creations earlier than heaven and earth.

Also, in Genesis 1.26, God says, "Let us make man in our image." Note the use of the plural "us." While there are benign explanations of the use of the plural here, there are other similar passages in Genesis that suggest there was a council of lesser gods attending on the Creator. These gods would (or, may) have been created before, "In the beginning."

In defense of "In the beginning," P may have meant, "In the beginning [of the creation of heaven and earth]." P may not have meant the beginning before which there was nothing because he may not have even conceived of nothing since until at least 1,000 years later man did not conceive of zero, a possible proxy for nothing.

Even the Greeks, with their advanced abilities in mathematics, did not conceive of zero; nor did the Romans, with their advanced ability in engineering. And the monk who in the mid 1st millennium CE created our current dating system clearly did not conceive of zero. He started what he thought was Jesus' birth year with 1, not 0, as would be our current usage. In other words, the monk thought Jesus' first birthday was the start of 2 CE. This led to our recent confusion and controversy over whether the 3rd millennium started on January 1st, 2000 or 2001.

So, to P, "In the beginning" may have been the same as, "When God began."

Christian Bibles probably use, "In the beginning," because that is the literal translation of the Greek Septuagint, *en arche*, and early translators of the Septuagint into Latin believed that the Bible was too sacred to alter. Thus, what may possibly have been an original mistranslation was perpetuated. Since the Evangelist John's Bible was undoubtedly the Septuagint, he may have used *en arche* for the opening of his Gospel: "In the beginning was the word."

Even granting that, "In the beginning," may have meant the same as, "When God began," to P, it does not mean the same to us, and translations are supposed to convey accurate understanding to those reading it. I prefer, "When God began," because that seems to me a more logical rendering of the text, and avoids the question of what may have existed before. Further, John's opening line to his Gospel poem is strong enough to stand on its own merits.

Appendix II

Comments on the Compilation of the Bible

The Hebrew Bible is composed of the *Torah* (Christian Pentateuch), the Prophets, and the Writings. In the hundreds of years following the destruction of the Temple in 70 CE, Jewish religious leaders proceeded to slowly agree on which of the Writings should be in the canon. There was no question about the *Torah*, it had been sanctioned many centuries earlier. There was also early consensus (according to most scholars) about the Prophets.

During the same early centuries CE, Christians were also slowly agreeing on a canon.

There are textual differences (mostly minor) between the Hebrew Bible and the Old Testament, but the most obvious difference is in the order of the books. The Hebrew Bible contains the Five Books of Moses (Greek Pentateuch, Hebrew *Torah*), the Prophets (Hebrew *Nevi'im*), and the Writings (Hebrew *Kethuvim*) in that order. The Hebrew Bible is also called the TANAKH, an approximate acronym of *Torah, Nevi'im,* and *Kethuvim*. The Old Testament reverses the order of the last two sections, ending with the Prophets.

It is difficult to judge which order is best. Until c 100 CE, the Jewish and Christian Bibles were written on scrolls, not in codices (the technical term for books; singular, codex), so each religion made its own decision as to order. By c. 100 CE, Christians preferred the codex, probably because they were more portable than scrolls and most services were held in homes. But codices (i.e., books) require a fixed order of the written material., which required a decision as to the order of the books, even though there was not widespread consensus as to the books that were to become the canon at that time.

Christians probably wanted the prophetic chapters closest to the New Testament (NT) to emphasize prophetic anticipation of Jesus.

Jews continued to use scrolls, probably since their worship was in a synagogue, a fixed building, and portability was not a necessity.

The order in both Bibles has no relationship to the date the individual books (and, sometimes, verses within books) were written. For example, it is generally accepted that Genesis 1 was written after Genesis 2 and 3. And, the prophet Amos is known to be the first written prophet, but his book is sixth in the order of the "Latter Prophets."

Of course, the NT suffers from the same deficiency; e.g., Paul's letters are published in the order of length,[57] not date written; further, these letters predate all of the Gospels, which come before Paul's writings in the NT. Of the gospels, Mark is generally considered to be earlier than Matthew, although Matthew precedes Mark in the NT.

1 and 2 Samuel and 1 and 2 Kings were each written as one book. They were separated only because they were too long to be written on one scroll.

As originally written, the Bible was not organized into chapters and verses. Chapters and verses were added by Christian scholars in the Middle Ages.

---

57. *The New Oxford Annotated Bible, New Revised Standard Version,* eds. Bruce M. Metzger and E. Roland Murphy (New York: Oxford University Press: 1991), 204, NT.

Sources and Additional Readings

Brown, Francis; Driver, S.R.; and Briggs, Charles A.; *The Brown-Driver-Briggs Hebrew and English Lexicon* (Boston: Houghton, Mifflin and Company: 1906).

Cameron, Ken "Rigor Without Mortis," *The American Fly Fisherman*, vol. 28, No 1.

Campbell, Antony F. and O'Brien, Mark A., *Sources of the Pentateuch*, (Minneapolis: Fortress Press: 1993).

Clifford, Richard J., *Creation Accounts in the Ancient Near East and in the Bible* (Washington, DC: The Catholic Biblical Quarterly Monograph Series 27, The Catholic Biblical Association of America: 1994).

Cooper, Jerrold S., "Cuneiform," *The Anchor Bible Dictionary* (ABD), David Noel Freedman, et. al., eds. (New York: Doubleday: 1992) Vol. 1.

Faulkner, William, *Requiem for a Nun*, (New York: New York: Random House: 1951).

Friedman, Richard Elliott, "Torah (Pentatuech)," ABD, Vol. 6.

Frymer-Kensky, Tikva, "Unwrapping the Torah," *Bible Review*, vol. XVIII, No. 5, Oct, 2002.

Hamilton, Victor, *The Book of Genesis Chapters 1–17* (Grand Rapids: Eerdmans Publishing Company: 1990)

Hendel, Ronald S., "Genesis, Book of," ABD, Vol. 2.

Lambert, W. G., "Enuma Elish," ABD, Vol. 2.

Tigay, Jeffrey H., "The Image of God and the Flood: Some New Developments," *Studies in Jewish Education and Judaica in Honor of Louis Newman*, (New York: KTAV Publishing House: 1984).

van Wolde, Ellen, *Stories of the Beginning* (Morehouse Publishing: 1995).

Westermann, Claus, *Genesis 1-11* (Minneapolis: Fortress Press: 1994).

Chapter 4

Origin of the Israelites in Judea

Archaeologists use the following "calendar" for the periods in and just before the time a significant population arose in the Judean Highlands, the area around Jerusalem:

- Late Bronze Age: c. 1550–1200 BCE
- Iron Age I: c. 1200—1000 BCE

The population of the Judean Highlands and areas east of the Jordan River increased from about 50,000 toward the end of the Late Bronze Age to about 150,000 at the end of Iron Age I, about 200 years later. This is an uneven and unconnected shaped area about one hundred miles from north to south by about seventy miles from east to west. The earlier population was concentrated in large villages and the later population in small settlements.[1]

This population growth among the group that became the Israelites cannot be explained by normal reproduction in the existing population. Who were they, and where did they come from?

The books of Exodus, Numbers, Joshua, and Judges provide a solution. They tell us that the increase came from the large number of Hebrews in the exodus from Egypt.

This answer was universally accepted until the early part of the last century. Both the Bible and Judeo-Christian tradition supported this answer to these questions. Few questioned the biblical account. It does account for the large population increase, and many Jews and Christians would like to believe the story of:

---

1. Stager, Lawrence E., in "Forging an Identity: The Emergence of Ancient Israel," *Oxford History of the Biblical World,* Michael Coogan, Editor (Oxford: Oxford University Press: 1998), 131, 134: "In...nine areas surveyed, eighty-eight Late Bronze Age sites" compare with 678 Iron Age I smaller settlements in the same area (see Appendix A). Finkelstein, Israel and Silberman, Neil, *The Bible Unearthed,* (New York: The Free Press: 2001) 115. Finkelstein and Silberman estimate a population of 45,000 and 250 sites c. 1200 BCE.

- the FLIGHT from Egypt as told in Exodus, Chapters 1 through 15.21;
- the WANDERING in the wildness as told from Exodus 15.22 through Exodus 19.2, and in Numbers, Chapters 13-14, 20-25, 31-33;[2] and
- the CONQUEST of the promised land as told in Joshua, Chapters 1 through 12 and Judges, Chapter 1.

It is certainly a fascinating and well-crafted story. Further, it seems completely original; i.e., I am aware of no prior Mesopotamian genre on which it could be based.

I will first outline and critique the biblical answers to these questions, and then briefly explore the other major theories explaining the origin of the Israelites in Judea. Here is the biblical story:

The Flight

As told in Exodus, 1-15

In the New Revised Standard Version of the Bible (NRSV), Exodus, Chapter 1, follows the Joseph story in Genesis 37-50 and says the, "sons of Israel" (Jacob) came to Egypt to join their brother Joseph escaping a famine in their land, and that they were well treated as relatives of Joseph, a powerful and trusted functionary in the Pharaoh's government.

After all the children of Jacob died, a new Pharaoh, fearing the strength of the growing Israelite population, imposed forced labor on them in hopes of curbing their growing influence. They were enslaved to build, "supply cities, Pithom and Rameses for Pharaoh. But the Israelites continued to, multipl[y] and spread, so that the Egyptians came to dread the Israelites."

Pharaoh ordered the midwives, Shiphrah and Puah, to kill all male

---

2. We focus here only on the journey narrative and do not include other important happenings during the wandering such as Moses' encounters with God, the giving of the commandments and the laws, etc.

infants, but, fearing God, they did not obey.

Chapter 2 tells of the miraculous birth story of Moses. Moses' mother hid him for three months and then left him in a basket at the riverbank; his sister Miriam watched at a distance. The Pharaoh's daughter found him and took him in. At the suggestion of Miriam, the Pharaoh's daughter agreed to use Moses' mother as a wet nurse.

The Pharaoh's daughter named him Moses because, "I drew him out of the water." The Hebrew word for Moses is written as the consonants, m-sh-h, is generally pronounced Moshe (mo-SHEH), and means "the one who draws (out)," perhaps a pun referring both to Moses' future mission to take his people out of Egypt and the circumstances of his adoption by the Pharaoh's daughter. The Egyptian noun equivalent is written as the consonants, m-s, and the verb equivalent, m-s-j, and means "to bear a child"[3] Vowels were not used in the written language of the Hebrew and Egyptian languages.

The Egyptian ms is common. For example, the Pharaoh Tuthmose's name (Tut-ms) means "Thoth is born," and the name Rameses (r'-ms-sw) means "Re is the one who gave him birth." The ending "s" in Moses, Rameses, etc. was added in the Greek Septuagint because "Greek does not permit masculine proper nouns to end in a vowel."[4]

The adult Moses killed an Egyptian overseer and fled to, "the land of Midian" (in modern northwestern Saudi Arabia), where he was taken in by a Midian priest named Jethro in Exodus (And Reuel and Hobab elsewhere).[5] He married the priest's daughter Zipporah and they had a son, Gershom.[6]

In Chapter 3, Moses is called by God in the burning bush to, "bring my people…out of Egypt." That is, to "draw out" his people. Moses asked God his name, and is told,

---

3. *The New Oxford Annotated Bible*, (NOAB) NRSV (Oxford et. al.: Oxford University Press, 1991), note to Exodus 2.10, 71.

4. Ogden Goellet, "Moses' Egyptian Name," *Bible Review*, June, 2004. 14.

5. Jethro in Exodus 3.1; 4.18; 18.1; Reuel in Numbers 10.29; Hobab in Judges 4.11.

6. From Hebrew ger, "alien." In Exodus 2.22, Moses says, "I have been an alien residing in a foreign land."

"I am who I am" (rendered in Hebrew as *"YHWH"*[7]), and

"This is my name forever, and this is my title for all generations."

God promised to give the Israelites, "a land overflowing with milk and honey…[the land] of the Canaanites, the Hittites, the Amorites, the Perizzites, the Hivites, and the Jebusites [inhabitants of Jerusalem]."[8]

Moses protested his lack of competence, but God insisted he complete his appointed task, and promised full support, and the help of his more eloquent older brother, Aaron.[9]

As planned, Moses and Aaron asked Pharaoh to release the Israelites. However, God hardened Pharaoh's heart, thus preventing Pharaoh from agreeing to release the Hebrews. God then punished Pharaoh with many plagues so that Pharaoh would know God's power.[10] After the final plague, the killing of all of the firstborn of Egypt, "from the firstborn of the Pharaoh who sat on his throne to the firstborn of the prisoner who was in the dungeon, and all the firstborn of the livestock."[11] Pharaoh relented and gave permission for the Israelites to leave Egypt. In

---

7. Which may be pronounced Yahweh. See note in NOAB to Exodus 3.14, 72, OT.

8. Exodus 3.8.

9. Moses was eighty years old and Aaron eighty-three when they spoke to Pharaoh. (Ex 7.7)

10. The plagues: the water in Egypt turned to blood; a swarm of frogs; gnats or lice; flies; a pestilence killing all animals; festering boils; hail which killed all animals in the fields; locusts; dense darkness; and finally, the killing of the firstborn of Egyptians and livestock. None of these plagues affected the Israelites; e.g., in the final plague the Lord passed over the homes of the Israelites, the origin of the Jewish holiday, Passover. There is a long-standing dispute about the fourth plague, which here is translated as flies. The Hebrew word is *arov*, which means a mixture. Early Rabbis debated whether that meant a mixture of animals or insects, and there were strong advocates of both. Gary Rendsburg in an article, "Beasts or Bugs," in *Bible Review*, April, 2003, makes the case for insects.

11. In addition to the livestock killed with the plague of the firstborn, the livestock had already been killed by pestilence in an earlier plague, "all the livestock of the Egyptians died." (Ex 9.6); and by the hail, "the hail struck down everything that was in the open field…both human and animal." (Ex 9.25) The author has the livestock killed three times. This is evidence that the sources for the plagues were various oral traditions that the author simply took in their entirety into his text.

11.2, God told Moses to tell the Israelites to,

"ask his neighbor for objects of silver and gold."

Then, in 12.35f,

"The Israelites had done as Moses told them; they had asked the Egyptians for jewelry of silver and gold, and for clothing, and the Lord had given the people favor in the sight of the Egyptians, so they let them have what they asked. And so they plundered the Egyptians."

So, after 430 years in Egypt (12.40), the Israelites left Egypt.

"God did not lead them by way of the land of the Philistines,…but, by the roundabout way of the wilderness toward the Red Sea." (13.17-18)

The Conquest Hypothesis requires a large body of invading Israelites to dislodge the Canaanite population. Thus,

"The Israelites journeyed from Rameses to Succoth, about six hundred thousand men on foot besides children. A mixed crowd also went with them and livestock in great numbers, both flocks and herds." (12.37f)

Of course, there were also women. It is probably not an exaggeration to assume that the total participation in the exodus, according to the Bible, exceeded two million. What followed was the escape through the parted "Red Sea" and the destruction of the Egyptian army as the waters returned.

The Greek text (the Septuagint) reads "Red Sea" but the Hebrew text reads "sea of reeds."[12] There are a number of shallow lakes with reeds in the area. One reason why the "sea of reeds" translation is so appealing is that it is a more logical explanation of the parting and flooding as reported in Exodus. In the shallow lakes, a strong windstorm will pile up the water on the side away from the wind. The water returns with a vengeance when the wind stops.

---

12. NOAB, note to Exodus 14.2, 86, OT.

Additional support for the translation "sea of reeds" is found in Exodus 14.25, "He clogged their chariot wheels so that they turned with difficulty." The floor of the Red Sea is packed sand. Anyone who has been to Daytona Beach, Florida, knows that automobiles can ride easily on this bed, as could chariots, which are much lighter than automobiles. But the floor of the shallow lakes is mud and would certainly clog the wheels of chariots.

Finally, the Red Sea is very deep. It can be over 7,700 feet deep. That is almost a mile and a half. To gain some prospective, it is comparable in depth to the Grand Canyon. The steep banks would make any passage on foot extremely difficult if not impossible.

In any event, the Egyptian army was destroyed. The Israelites then entered the wilderness of the Sinai desert.

Wandering in the Wilderness

As told in Exodus, Chapters 15–19; and in Numbers, Chapters 13–14, 20–25, 31–33[13]

In Exodus 20, during the Wandering in the Wilderness, the Lord gave the commandments to Moses on Mount Sinai (Ex 20, 24 and Deut. 4), whose location remains unknown. As Professor Jon Levenson of Harvard writes, "We know nothing about Sinai, but an immense amount about the traditions concerning Sinai."[14]

In Numbers 13.1, "The Lord said to Moses, 'Send men to spy out the land of Canaan which I am giving to the Israelites.' The spies returned and reported, 'We are not able to go up against this people, for they are stronger than we.'"

In Numbers 14, "the Israelites cried, wept, and complained, saying, 'Let us choose a captain, and go back to Egypt.' The Lord then condemned them for their faithlessness and sentenced them to wander for

---

13. The other chapters in Exodus, Leviticus, and Numbers are concerned with laws and genealogies, which do not concern us here. Deuteronomy has three speeches by Moses and ends with his death.

14. Jon D. Levenson, *Sinai and Zion* (New York: HarperSanFrancisco: 1985), 17.

forty years in the wilderness, and there they shall die."

Numbers 20 makes it clear that the Israelites camped at Kadesh (identified as Kadesh-barnea in Numbers 34) for almost all of the forty years of wanderings. Kadesh is near the current border between Israel and Egypt. When it came time to leave Kadesh, the Israelites asked the king of Edom for permission to cross his land. He refused, so the Israelites turned away.

In Numbers 21, the Canaanite king of Arad, "who lived in the Negev, attacked the Israelites and took some of them captive. The Lord handed over the Canaanites [the people of Arad]; and they [the Israelites] utterly destroyed them and their towns". The Israelites then took Heshbon, in Ammon, and Dibon, in Moab. In Moab, the Israelites prepared to cross the Jordan and take the land promised them by the Lord.

The Conquest

As told in Joshua, Chapters 1-12 and Judges, Chapter 1

In Joshua 1, God said to Joshua:

> "Now proceed to cross the Jordan, you and all this people, into the land that I am giving to them, to the Israelites. Every place that the sole of your foot will tread upon I have given to you, as I promised to Moses. From the wilderness and the Lebanon as far as the great river, the river Euphrates, all the land of the Hittites, to the Great Sea in the west shall be your territory."

Joshua then organized all the Israelite tribes including the warriors from, "the Reubenites, the Gadites, and the half tribe of Manasseh," whose allotted land was east of the Jordan River and had already been conquered. Thus, all the tribes participated in conquering each tribe's allotted land, resulting in the so-called unified conquest.

In Joshua 6, Joshua and the Israelites, with God's help, proceed to conquer all the land promised by God, beginning with Jericho. At God's instruction, they marched once around Jericho's walls for six days with trumpets blowing. On the seventh day, they marched around seven times, and, at Joshua's command, they shouted with the trumpets blowing, "and the walls fell down flat; so the people charged straight ahead into the city and captured it. They then devoted to destruction by the edge of the sword all in the city, both men and women, young and old, oxen, sheep, and donkeys."

All were killed except the woman, Rahab, who helped the Israelite spies, and her family. In Joshua 8, the next target was Ai, "The Lord said to Joshua…"You shall do to Ai and its king as you did to Jericho and its king." And, the results were similar, "The total of those who fell that day, both men and women, was twelve thousand—all the people of Ai."

In Joshua, Chapter 10, the Israelites battled the warriors and kings of Jerusalem, Hebron, Jarmuth, Lachish, and Eglon, "until they were wiped out, and the kings executed."Joshua then, "Took Makkedah… and…he utterly destroyed every person in it, including the king." The cities of Libnah, Gezer, and Debir suffered the same fate.

> "So Joshua defeated the whole land, the hill country and the Negev and the lowland and the slopes, and all their kings; he left no one remaining,, but utterly destroyed all that breathed, as the Lord God commanded."

In Joshua 11, Joshua and the Israelites defeated Hazor, Madon, Shimron, Achshaph, the Canaanites, the Hittites, the Perizzites, the Jebusites (inhabitants of Jerusalem), the Hivites, and the Anakim in the hill country; they killed their kings and all their people.

Joshua 12 lists the 31 kings defeated and killed by Joshua in his campaign to take the land promised to the Israelites by God.

Joshua,13-23 deals with the allotment of land to the tribes. Chapter 24 contains the covenant at Shechem, which probably stems from a very early oral tradition.[15]

Altogether, the book of Joshua, with its extensive killing—even genocide—of the "other" reveals "the dark side of tribalism."[16]

Judges 1 continues the conquest story with several inconsistencies. For

---

15. In Joshua 24.6, "When I brought your ancestors out of Egypt," there is no reference to the events on Mt. Sinai. Thus, it may predate the writing of Exodus.

16. A comment by Ronald Hendel at an Oxford University seminar in 1999, sponsored by the Biblical Archeological Society.

example: In Joshua 12, it identifies the king of Jerusalem (v 10), among those killed by Joshua and the Israelites (v 7); and the land of the Jebusites (inhabitants of Jerusalem) as land given to one of the tribes.

- In Judges 1.8, there is a seeming confirmation, which fails to give credit to Joshua, "The people of Judah fought against Jerusalem and took it. They put it to the sword and set the city on fire."
- Then, in Judges 1.21 we read a contradiction to Judges 1.8, and Joshua 12, "But the Benjaminites did not drive out the Jebusites who lived in Jerusalem; so the Jebusites have lived in Jerusalem among the Benjaminites to this day."
- And Joshua 15.63, supporting Judges 1.21, reads, "But the people of Judah, could not drive out the Jebusites, the inhabitants of Jerusalem; so the Jebusites live with the people of Judah in Jerusalem to this day."

Of perhaps greater interest is the fact that Judges does not portray a unified conquest, as does Joshua. In Judges 1, each tribe sets out to conquer their own allotted land.

For example,

- Judah, with Simeon, conquered their allotted land,
- as did Joseph, but
- Manasseh, Ephraim, Asher, and Naphtali failed to drive out the indigenous population in their allotted land, and lived among them, and, "The Amorites pressed the Danites (the tribe of Dan) back into the hill country."

Judges 2 states the general procedure,

"When Joshua dismissed the people, the Israelites all went to their own inheritances to take possession of the land."

Obviously, according to the text, some were more successful than others. But the main point is that they did not attempt to take over their lands as a cooperative group, but acted separately, unlike the way the conquest was accomplished in Joshua.

These discrepancies in the biblical text indicate the likely source of the various stories as different oral traditions that were all preserved.

That is a brief synopsis of the biblical story of the Exodus, Wandering in the Wilderness, and Conquest.

There is almost unanimous agreement among biblical scholars and archaeologists in dating the story time of these events in the mid to late 13th century—probably during the time of the Pharaoh, Rameses II (called, Rameses the Great), who, according to many scholars, reigned from 1290–1224, but, according to other scholars, reigned from 1279–1213—a total of sixty-six years in any event. Scholarly support for dating the story time of the Exodus in the mid to late 13th century includes the following:

1. In Exodus 1.11, "they built supply cities, Pithom and Rameses for Pharaoh." These projects may have taken place during the reign of Rameses II.[17]

2. Many of the names, including Moses and the mid-wives named in Exodus 1.15, "are characteristic of the Ramesside era."[18]

3. The final plague visited by God on the Egyptians was the killing of all firstborn, including the son of the Pharaoh. Rameses II's eldest son and crown prince died between 1259 and 1249 BCE.[19]

4. The favorable political, social, and material conditions for the appearance of Israel in Canaan in around 1200 BCE further supports the assumption among most scholars that the story-time of the exodus occurred in the middle of the 13th century."[20]

---

17. Frank J. Yurco, "Merenptah's Canaanite Campaign and Israel's Origins" in *Exodus: The Egyptian Evidence,* Ernest Frerichs and Leonard Lesko, Editors (Winona Lake, IN: Eisenbrauns, Inc., 1997) 46.

18. Ibid. p. 46 f.

19. Ibid. p. 47 f.

20. Nahum M. Sarna, "Book of Exodus" in *The Anchor Bible Dictionary* (ABD), Vol. 2 (David Noel Freedman, et. al., eds. (New York: Doubleday: 1992), 696. This refers to the invasions of the Sea Peoples and the lessening of Egyptian power in Canaan.

Critique: The Flight

Many of the elements of this story have historic credibility.

1. It is virtually certain that there were people from Palestine in the Egyptian Delta, many of whom came, like Jacob's sons in the story, to avoid the famines in Palestine, which occurred periodically.[21] There is, "an analogy in Papyrus Anastasi VI, in which a frontier official reports on the passage of Edomite Bedouin tribes…into the delta of Egypt 'to keep them and their cattle alive.'"[22]
2. The name Moses, and the names of the midwives, Shiphrah and Puah, are common Egyptian names of the Late Bronze period, the commonly accepted story time of the Exodus.
3. Many of the biblical plagues occurred naturally in Egypt from time to time. For example, the Nile would run red if there had been heavy rains in Ethiopia, and the red clay there was carried down the Nile to Egypt. Frogs would leave the river if the flood was too high. Gnats, flies and locusts were common. Sandstorms could bring darkness. And Rameses II's Crown Prince, "the firstborn of the Pharaoh," died around the story time of the flight.
4. "The conscription of Israelites for work on state projects (Exod. 1.11) correlates with the tradition preserved by Diodorus Siculus that Rameses II preferred to conscript foreigners rather than Egyptians for his vast building programs."[23]

But there are problems: "Exodus 12.37-38 reports that 600,000 Hebrews of fighting age left Egypt. This number plus their wives and children along with the mixed multitude said to accompany them would have totaled some two and a half million. Marching ten abreast, the numbers would have formed a line over 150 miles long and would have required

---

21. Ibid., 697.
22. Ibid.
23. Ibid.

eight or nine days to march by any fixed point."²⁴ Further, a total of even two million would be about half the population of Egypt at that time.²⁵

Even accounting for exaggeration in the numbers leaving Egypt, one would expect some Egyptian records of this most unusual story. The exodus of a large number of the workforce should have appeared in the official records of the Egyptians. But, to date, the history of the Israelites in Egypt has gone totally unnoticed in the Egyptian records that have been recovered. One reason for this lack of record of the Israelites is that the Egyptians referred to all peoples from Canaan as "Asians." This is an indication of the indifference shown to foreigners by the Egyptians, even though they were in total control of Canaan and must have been aware of the variety of peoples there.

The earliest mention of "Israel" by the Egyptians is on the Merneptah Stele, a stone monument dated between 1220 and 1209 BCE, and those Israelites were not in Egypt. "Israel" in the Merneptah stele refers to a people and not a state or location.²⁶ While it is true that a new discovery could overturn the current emptiness of supporting evidence, it is significant that the substantial records now available include only one incident of two people identified as "Asians" escaping into the desert. This occurred during the reign of the same Merneptah of the stele, who succeeded his father, Rameses II as Pharaoh sometime between 1224 and 1213 BCE. These "Asians" may have been Israelites, but they could also have been any of the other peoples from Canaan.²⁷

---

24. Maxwell J. Miller and John H. Hayes, *A History of Ancient Israel and Judah* (Philadelphia: The Westminster Press: 1986), 60.

25. Figures on an axe head c. 3200 BCE report the population as c. 1.4 million at that time. Roman records in early CE report the population as c. seven million. Thus, the population c. 1250 is estimated at c. four million.

26. We know it was a people because the Egyptian language uses "determinatives" which are hieroglyphs placed at the end of a word revealing the type of that word. In the Merneptah stele, the determinative after "Israel" identifies the word as describing a "people," not a place or state.

27. Nahum M. Sarna, "Israel in Egypt" in *Ancient Israel,* Hershel Shanks, ed. (Washington: Biblical Archaeological Society: 1999), 39. Sarna tells of the escape of two "Asians" (recorded in the Papyrus Anastasi 5) and reports "Asians" coming to Egypt to obtain water and food during a drought/famine.

Some of the elements of the biblical story, while not impossible, are certainly unlikely. For example, in Exodus, Moses meets with Pharaoh many times. Would a Pharaoh meet with a commoner, especially a non-Egyptian, even once, much less eleven times? Moses' birth story also contains many improbable elements:

a. The Pharaoh orders only two midwives, Shiprah and Puah, to kill infant males. Clearly, two midwives to serve an adult female population even substantially smaller than claimed would be completely inadequate.

b. It seems most unlikely that the Pharaoh's daughter would save a Hebrew male infant after her father had ordered the midwives to kill them.

c. The Pharaoh's daughter's use of the name Moses itself creates difficulties. The translation from the Hebrew, "one who draws (out)," would be closer to the biblical report if it were the passive, "one drawn (out)." The Egyptian translation, "to beget a child" seems irrelevant to the text, but are we to believe the Pharaoh's daughter knew Hebrew?

d. It seems unlikely that Moses' mother failed to provide him a name. Perhaps it was m-sh-h, and perhaps the Pharaoh's daughter accepted it because it seemed to have had an Egyptian counterpart. But why did the Yahwist author (J) tell us it was the name given by the Pharaoh's daughter? Would not J have wanted to use a Hebrew name provided by the mother (or father)? All other Hebrew heroes have such names. Why not the greatest hero of them all?

e. J names the two midwives, and Moses' sister (Miriam), but fails to provide a name for the Pharaoh's daughter or Moses' mother. More importantly, while J provides a father for Joshua, "son of Nun"[28] he fails to provide a name for Moses' father. P, however, does provide the names for Moses' father and mother in

---

28. E.g., Numbers 11.28.

Exodus 6.20, Amram and Jochebed, But P wrote after J, and the questions remain, did J leave out the names of Moses' parents, or did the redactor (a later editor) delete them; and what were P's sources for the names he provides? While the Pharaoh is also unnamed, that oversight may have been deliberate and intended to resonate with the experience of those who ultimately became Israelites and had been oppressed by different Pharaohs over many years in different locations.

In sum, some aspects of the flight story could be historical, but it is clear that the number leaving Egypt is greatly exaggerated. Archaeologist Frank Yurco suggested in a lecture in October, 2002, at the Oriental Institute of the University of Chicago, that possibly 6,000 would be a more credible number. But we are going to run into difficulties with even a number that large in the next section, the Wandering in the Wilderness.

Critique: Wandering in the Wilderness

We now find many reasons to question the historical accuracy of the biblical account:

1. There is not a shred of archeological evidence for a large group of people passing through the Sinai desert at any time in the past: "Not even a single shard [a piece of broken pottery], no structure, not a single house, no evidence of an ancient encampment." The desert is an ideal preserver of artifacts and, for example, "discloses evidence for pastoral activity in [the Sinai in] the third millennium BC." The area has been combed over and over again, including sites clearly identifiable from the biblical account. For example, "the children of Israel camped at Kadesh-barnea for thirty-eight of the forty years of wanderings… The general location of this place is clear [from the description in Numbers 34]…Yet repeated excavations and surveys throughout the entire area have not provided even the slightest evidence for activity in the Late Bronze

Age, not even a single shard."[29] There has been no success in verifying the biblical account of the wandering in the wilderness story by archeologists who were attempting to prove the accuracy of the biblical account as well as those with no preconceived agenda; Jewish, Christian, and agnostic archaeologists alike have turned up no artifacts to support the story told in Exodus and Numbers.

2. The logistics of supporting a large group—even one much smaller than claimed—for forty years in the desert would have been impossible. Think of the demands for food and water in an area with limited supplies of these necessities, and the need for immense sanitary facilities.

3. Recall the story in Numbers 20.14f about the confrontation with the king of Edom. But Edom was almost empty in the Late Bronze Age, and there was certainly no king. Edom did not become a state until the 8th or 7th century BCE when the Assyrians established a kingdom there to facilitate their trade.[30]

4. We are told that the Canaanite king of Arad attacked the Israelites and took some of them captive, yet, "Almost twenty years of intensive excavations at the site of tel Arad…have revealed remains of a great Early Bronze Age city…and an Iron Age fort, but no remains whatsoever from the Late Bronze Age, when the place was apparently deserted… Arad simply did not exist in the Late Bronze Age."[31]

5. As to the alleged conquest in the Wilderness of Heshbon and Dibon in the Transjordan, archaeological excavations in both locations "showed that there was no Late Bronze Age city, not

---

29. Israel Finkelstein and Neil Silberman, *The Bible Unearthed* (New York: The Free Press: 2001), 63. Numbers 34 locates Kadesh-barnea where the Israelites camped for thirty-eight of the forty years of wandering as the modern oasis, En el-Qudeirat where only the ruins of a 7th century BCE fort have been found. Also Ezion-geber is cited as another campground where only Late Iron Age material has been found.

30. Finkelstein and Silberman, 68. Also, see their Appendix A, on page 22 for the number of settlements in Edom in the Late Bronze Age.

31. Ibid., 64.

even a small village there; [they were] very sparsely inhabited in the Late Bronze Age… [M]ost parts of this region…were not even inhabited by a sedentary population at that time."[32]

The biblical story of the Wandering in the Wilderness is severely compromised and gives evidence of being either written or extensively redacted in the 7th or 6th century BCE, when the areas discussed were actually inhabited.

Critique: The Conquest

1. Extensive archaeological activity clearly proves that the lists of conquests in Joshua, like those previously seen in the Wandering in the Wilderness in Numbers, do not conform to the reality of what archaeologists have found. Archeologists, most notably Kathleen Kenyon in the late 1940s and early 1950s, determined that Jericho was unoccupied, except for a possibly small settlement in the 13th century BCE. And, as to the famous walls of Jericho, "there is no archeological data to support the presence of a walled town," and, "a study of the settlement pattern of the LB [Late Bronze] sites in Canaan shows that only eight of the seventy-six known settlements were fortified."[33] Egypt was in control of Canaan during this period, and was undoubtedly sensitive to the possibility of revolt, since Egypt had only recently expelled their former rulers, the Hyksos, into Canaan. Canaanite cities were not permitted to build fortification walls. The Egyptians wanted them to be more vulnerable to the force of the Egyptian army.

    The alleged victory at Ai is also impossible. The ruins at Ai stemmed from the Early Bronze Age (c 2500 BCE); and the site was unoccupied from then until a small Iron Age I village arose. This small village was not built until about one hundred years

---

32. Ibid. Also see their Appendix A on page 22 indicating that no settlements have been found in Moab in the Late Bronze Age.
33. Netzer, Ehud, "Jerico," in ABD, vol. III 736.

after the Israelites allegedly passed through. Noted scholar Martin Noth held that "the Ai account in Joshua 8 is legendary and etiological in nature, and is therefore unhistorical."[34]

2. Even where Late Bronze ruins seem to support these conquest stories, archeology has on some occasions led us to different conclusions. Thus, Lachish was destroyed in the 13th century during the story time of Joshua. In Joshua 10.32, "The Lord gave Lachish into the hands of Israel, and he took it…and struck it with the edge of the sword, and every person in it," but, an Egypto-Canaanite settlement was its replacement, not an Israelite one.[35] There have been many other archeological discoveries that have undermined the biblical version of the conquest.

3. The conquests do not even conform to the claims in other biblical verses and books. As previously noted, Judges 1.21 and Joshua 15.63 contradict both Judges 1.8 and Joshua 12 with respect to the taking of Jerusalem and the killing of its king and inhabitants. 2 Samuel 4.7 has Jerusalem finally taken by David seven years into his reign, 200 years or more after Joshua allegedly crossed the Jordan and began the conquest (see Appendix IV for more details).

4. Also, the land promised to the Israelites by God in Joshua 1.2 is idealized and includes land never under Israel's control. For example, Israel never controlled, "all the land of the Hittites,"[36] never controlled all the land to, "the Great Sea in the west," and never controlled most of the land east of the Jordan to, "the great river, the river Euphrates."

5. At the story time of the conquest, the Egyptians were on the verge of withdrawing from Canaan but were still a dominant force in

---

34. Joseph A. Calloway, "Ái," in ABD, see Appendix B in Vol. I, 130. Etiological, in the sense of explaining the presence of ruins at Ai by attributing them to Joshua.

35. Stager, 131.

36. *Cuneiform Parallels to the Old Testament*, Robert W. Rogers, trans. and ed. (The Abingdon Press, New York and Cincinnatti: 1912) 260: "The name of 'Hittites' is used in the Bible in a very wide sense…also covering a subordinate clan settled in southern Palestine about Heron."

Canaan for at least the following seventy-five years.[37] The reign of Rameses III (1186-1154 BCE) is memorialized in Papyrus Harris I, which is 143 feet long. In this extensive record, neither the Israelites/Hebrews nor an exodus are mentioned. But there is evidence of Egyptian influence in Canaan in the form of claims of military prisoners from campaigns in Canaan at that time. For example,

"I have brought back in great numbers those that my sword has spared, with their hands tied behind their backs before my horses."[38]

This is confirmed by hieroglyphs and other archaeological evidence at an Egyptian stronghold at Beth-shean south of the Sea of Galillee dating from the reign of Rameses III. Also, "The ancient Canaanite city of Mediggo disclosed evidence for strong Egyptian influence as late as the days of Rameses VI, who ruled toward the end of the twelfth century BCE. This was long after the supposed conquest of Canaan by the Israelites."[39] Any move by any other military organization would have been opposed by the Egyptian authorities and army, and we can safely assume that the better trained and equipped Egyptian army would have made short work of the Israelites as suggested by Papyrus Harris I. In any event, the presence and opposition by the occupying Egyptians at least should have been noted and commented on by Joshua. Yet there is no mention of an Egyptian presence in the books of Joshua or Judges. There are at least two possible explanations for this oversight:

a. Recall from the previous chapter that myth, unlike history, selects its sources and ignores those that are inconvenient for its purposes. Acknowledging Egyptian control of Canaan would certainly take the wind out of the campaign to raise Joshua's stature to that of a superhero.

---

37. Amihai Mazar, *Archaeology, The Land of the Bible, 10,000-586 B.C.E.* (New York: Doubleday, 1990), 288.

38. Ronald S. Hendel, "Exodus: A Book of Memories," *Bible Review*, Vol. XVIII, no 4, August, 2002, 41.

39. Finkelstein and Silberman, 78f.

b. The books of Joshua and Judges were probably written in the 7th and 6th centuries; the authors may have been unaware of Egypt's domination during the story time of the Exodus. It is likely that their sources were primarily oral, and, as we all know, stories improve with age—details disappear or become exaggerated, and heroes take on epic proportions.

6. Many people today would question a direct verbal encounter between God and any human. In Exodus, Leviticus, and Numbers the Lord speaks to Moses over 140 times. In most cases, the Lord's statement is preceded by, "Then the Lord said to Moses." In many cases, this statement punctuates a continuing monologue by the Lord.[40]

Deuteronomy contains three addresses from Moses to the Israelites recalling the words of the Lord, but includes no direct spoken words from God to Moses or anyone else.

The book of Joshua has God speaking to Joshua ten times.[41]

In sum, in the four books of Exodus, Leviticus, Numbers and Joshua, the Lord speaks to Israelite leaders well over 150 times. In the New Testament Gospels, as certain as they are about Jesus' close relationship to God, God explicitly speaks to Jesus only at Jesus' baptism (probably unheard by others), at the Transfiguration (heard only by Peter, James and John), and possibly in Jerusalem, although the crowd hears it as thunder (John 12.28-28).

7. "No extant non-biblical records make reference to Moses or the exodus, therefore the question of historicity depends solely on the evaluation of the biblical accounts,"[42] which, as we have seen, seem generally unreliable.

---

40. For example, the Lord speaks to Moses in Exodus alone at least fifty-six times: 3.4, 4.19, 4.21, 6.1, 6.2, 6.10, 6.28, 7.1, 7.8, 7.14, 8.1, 8.16, 8.20, 9.1, 9.8, 9.13, 9.22, 10.1, 10.12, 10.21, 11.1, 11.9, 12.1, 12.43, 13.1, 14.1, 14.15, 14.26, 16.4, 16.11, 16.28, 17.5, 17.14, 19.3, 19.10, 19.21, 20.1, 20.22, 24.1, 24.12, 25.1, 30.11, 30.17, 30,22, 30.34, 31.1, 31.12, 32.7, 32.9, 33.1, 33.14, 33.17, 34.1, 34.10, 34.27, and 40.1. In Leviticus the Lord speaks to Moses thirty-three times, and in Numbers, fifty-five times.

41. Joshua 1.1, 3.7, 4.2, 5.2, 6.2, 7.10, 8.1, 11.6, 13.1, 20.1.

42. Florence Morgan Gillman, "Moses" ABD, Vol. 4, 909.

8. There is extensive and persuasive archaeological, literary, and theological evidence that the books of Deuteronomy, Joshua, and Judges (and Kings I and II, and Samuel I and II) were written by the same school of theologians in 7th and perhaps 6th century BCE Judah, roughly 400 years after the alleged events. This school of authors is called the Deuteronomist (D), with the following archeological and theological markers:

- Archaeologically, many of the conquest sites in Joshua/Judges were not occupied until well after the conquest story time, but these sites were established before the 7th century, in time for D to be aware of them.

- Theologically, in Judges, "the tribes…Judah and Simeon perfectly fulfilled their sacred mission in conquering all the Canaanite cites in their territories," and killing all their inhabitants. This was the area that became Judah, the home of the pious and reformist Kings Hezekiah and Josiah, where D wrote. "The kingdom of Judah was therefore protected from the immediate danger of idolatry in its midst. But this was not the case with the tribes that later comprised the core of the northern kingdom of Israel. All of them…failed…to eliminate the Canaanites…No wonder then that pious Judah survived [the onslaught of the Assyrians in the 8th century BCE, but not the Babylonians in the early 6th century BCE] and apostate Israel was vanquished [by the Assyrians in 720 BCE]. Indeed, most of the tales of the book of Judges deal with the sin and punishment of the northern tribes. Not a single story explicitly accuses Judah of idolatry."[43]

"It is clear that this theological interpretation of the tales in the book of Judges was developed centuries after the events it purportedly describes."[44]

Thus, like the wandering in the wilderness story, the conquest story is severely compromised.

---

43. Finkeltein and Silberman, 121.
44. Ibid., 120.

For these and other reasons, I believe the biblical account of the Exodus—the flight, the wandering in the wilderness, and the conquest as reported in Exodus, Numbers, Joshua and Judges—is a myth and does not represent reliable history. This is also the position officially accepted by The United Synagogues of Conservative Judaism in their *Torah* and Commentary, *Etz Hayim,* (Tree of Life in Hebrew), published in 2001.

There are important historical realities contained in the myths. For example:

a. The Egyptians certainly used slaves/forced labor in the construction of their projects. This is confirmed by the 14th century BCE Armana letters to and from the Pharaohs[45] and the previously mentioned quote from the 12th century BCE Harris Papyrus I written as a tribute to Rameses III. Also, apparently, Rameses II preferred using foreign conscripts (see page 85).

b. Canaanites would have related to the stories about slavery in Egypt since they were not only subject to being sent to Egypt as slaves, but were also oppressed by the Egyptians in Canaan.

In addition, there may be other realities buried in the myths. For example:

c. It is possible that some of the Israelites did migrate from Egypt to the Judean Highlands (though not in sufficient numbers to explain the large population increase from Late Bronze to Iron Age I). They may have moved rapidly across the desert in small groups over a period of about 200 years. In any event, they would have been a distinct minority of the population in Judah.

d. It is possible that, "A historical figure named Moses may have been transformed into the savior and mediator of all Israel perhaps generalized from the memory of a small group."[46]

---

45. *The Tel—Armana Tablets,* Samuel A. B. Mercer, ed. (Toronto: The Macmillan Company of Canada Limited, 1939), vol. I xv. "All the tablets except three are in the Akkadian language...[and, the Akkadian phonetic script] was internationally used in writing not only Akkadian but other languages as well."

46. Hendel, 51.

Myths do tell stories that convey universal truths important to the community.[47] Christians see the parables of Jesus in the New Testament Gospels as conveyers of universal truths important to the Christian community. The Prodigal Son parable tells of the boundless nature of God's love. The parable of the Good Samaritan gives us a glimpse of the neighbor we are asked to love. These two along with many others give us a vital insight into Jesus' conception of the Kingdom of God. Are these parables historically accurate? Did the events portrayed actually happen? Probably not. Parables are a form of myth. Even though they may not be historically accurate, they do tell us the truth. The same is true of the myths told in Exodus, Numbers, Joshua, and Judges.

The Exodus myth reveals two truths meaningful to all communities in all times:

1. mankind seeks freedom from slavery, and
2. mankind seeks a safe place to live of one's own, free of control by others.

For Christians and Jews, these truths supplement God's gift of freedom of will. In our culture "slavery" can be imposed by:

- abusive persons (including verbal and physical abuse, domestic and other)
- abusive employers,
- abusive governments,
- mental or emotional problems (including addictions).

Passover is the wonderful Jewish celebration of freedom from forced labor in Egypt and freedom in general.

God's assistance in the Exodus text comes with a price. Freedom of will does not include freedom from accountability to God. In Exodus

---

47. Most of us have experienced finding truth in a work of fiction that was not historically accurate.

4.23, God tells Moses to give this message to Pharaoh, "Let my son [Israel] go that he may worship me." Note that the author of this passage (J) does not say, "so he will be free." The authors and redactors of Exodus were primarily interested in their covenantal relationship with Yahweh and not about the global messages we look for today. If the Israelites did not use their freedom of will to worship and obey God in accordance with his dictates, they were held accountable, and much of the Books of Samuel and Kings tell of D's firmly held belief of the inevitable consequences of their disobedience.

Note also that in the exodus, wandering, and conquest stories, God is not concerned with the fate of the Egyptian soldiers and the various peoples wiped out in the taking of the Promised Land. The authors of these passages were members of a tribe; i.e., viewed other peoples as "others" (recall footnote 16, where Ronald Hendel refers to these slaughters as "the dark side of tribalism"). At the time these oral traditions originated, Yahweh *(YHWH)* was the tribe's god, and only concerned with the welfare of Israelites. Later on, when Yahweh became a universal god, later authors saw Yahweh as caring also for "the nations" (*goyim*, gentiles).[48]

Many of us may not see the disasters that plagued Israel and Judah as connected to disobedience of the rules in the *Torah* (more about that in Chapter 5).

There are other truths imbedded in the myths. For example, it is clear that the Wandering in the Wilderness for forty years story is not credible and has no historical basis. The number forty is a traditional number in the Bible and probably simply means a long time. For example, in Genesis 7.4, J's God tells Noah, "I will send rain on the earth for forty days and forty nights." And in Mark 1.13, Jesus, was "in the wilderness forty days." I think the truth this part of the myth conveys is that the struggle for freedom can be hazardous, require courage, and can take a long time, as the Israelites in the story discovered in the Sinai desert, and the modern day Israelis and Palestinians have found in the 20th and 21st centuries.

Freedom from slavery may be part of what we call salvation. The

---

48. See, e.g., Amos 9. 7, Isaiah 2.2-4, and Jonah 3 and 4.

drive for freedom and a safe place to live has always been a primary goal for mankind.

Returning to our principal questions, we now believe the majority of people who became Israelites did not come from Egypt. So, who were they? And where did they come from? Here are some possible answers to these questions from well-known scholars.[49]

The Pastoral Nomad Hypothesis

In 1925, German scholar Albrecht Alt rejected the biblical account of the Unified Conquest and theorized that semi-nomadics who had rotated seasonally into the sparsely populated Judean highlands became permanent residents. Alt had access to the Armana letters—written to and from Canaanite kings to their master the Pharaoh in the 14th century BCE—which indicated that the Lowlands were densely populated but the Highlands were not.

According to Alt, the ebbing of Egyptian power in Canaan in Iron Age I made it possible for the nomads to settle permanently in the sparsely populated Highlands. He was joined in this theory by the equally eminent German scholar Martin Noth. To publish such a thesis required courage at that time. One can only imagine the hostility they received from those defending the historical integrity of the Bible.

The Pastoral Nomad Hypothesis has attractive elements, especially in regard to the difference in population density between the Lowlands and the Highlands and the ebbing power of Egypt in the area during Iron Age I—an ebbing that probably began shortly after the story time of the biblical Exodus and Conquest. The Highlands of Judea may have been an area of early Egyptian withdrawal because of its relative insignificance. But, as previously noted, the Egyptians were still a force in Canaan as late as the reign of Rameses IV at the end of the 12th century BCE. Nevertheless, a slow increase in the population of the Highlands by nomads who were not a military threat might have been ignored by the Egyptian authorities.

---

49. Sources for the following material on alternate hypotheses include class notes from the University of Chicago and Stager, p. 137f.

One can also speculate that the Pastoral Nomad Hypothesis finds an interesting echo in the Bible. Remember that it was in the desert that Moses first encountered Yahweh when he was living in Midian with Jethro, the priest of the unnamed god. Later, in Exodus 18, Jethro visited Moses during the wandering, praised Yahweh for "deliver [ing Moses] from the Egyptians and the Pharaoh…brought a burnt offering and sacrifices to God,…[and ate] in the presence of God." Is it possible that Jethro was a priest of Yahweh, and that Yahweh was brought to the Judean Highland by the nomads?

Both the Biblical Conquest and the Pastoral Nomad Hypotheses postulate an external source of migration.

Critique

The Pastoral Nomad Hypothesis is a more credible solution than the Conquest Hypothesis. But the limited nomadic population cannot account for the population increase of about 100,000 between the Late Bronze Age and the end of Iron Age I. It is unfair to be overly critical of the work of Alt and Noth because they were without the benefit of the recent archeological findings that determined the large increase in population in the Highlands from the Late Bronze Age to Iron Age I. The desert nomad population was simply not large enough to account for the population increase that archaeological evidence indicates.

We know the nomad population was limited because the Late Bronze Age preceded the use of camels, which were not in wide use until the end of Iron Age I, about 1000 BCE. Thus, the desert nomads of the Late Bronze Age were not deep desert Bedouins with camels; they had only donkeys as beasts of burden and were required to cluster around oases since donkeys had to be constantly near a supply of water. This severely limited the area in the desert that could support a group; thus, the desert nomads were limited to a relatively small population at that time.

The Pastoral Nomad Hypothesis does not solve the mystery, although there is no reason to exclude the possibility that some nomads from modern northwest Saudi Arabia did settle in the empty Judean Highlands and perhaps even introduced the worship of Yahweh there.

The Peasant Revolt Hypothesis

An American scholar, George Mendenhall, presented his theory in "The Hebrew Conquest of Palestine," an article in Biblical Archaeologist 25 (1962). He believed that at the close of the Late Bronze Age, idealistic Canaanite peasants, motivated by a belief in Yahweh and egalitarianism, revolted against their masters and joined a group of former slaves led by Moses in the Highlands.

Another American, Norman K. Gottwald revised the theory in his book, *The Tribes of Yahweh*, published in 1979. Gottwald saw, "the origins of Israel in the commingling of a heterogeneous collection of disaffected social elements inside Canaan. These groups rebelled against the entire existing sociopolitical and religious feudal system, gradually retribalized, and developed a new social order along egalitarian lines based on a covenant relationship with *YHWH*."[50] Like Alt and Noth, Mendenhall and Gottwald were also unaware of the large population increase in the Judean Highlands during Iron Age I.

Critique

As we shall see, the source for most of the increase in the population (i.e., Canaan) in this theory is probably correct, and it is possible that a sufficient number of revolutionaries could have populated the Judean Highlands. But Mendenhall's and Gottwald's theories have at least three difficulties:

1. The lowland residents were not real peasants (i.e., generally neither bound to the land, nor tenant farmers); they were owners of small plots, mixing farming with pasturing small herds and flocks of animals.

2. Although there is evidence that the Iron Age Israelites in the Judean Highlands favored egalitarianism,[51] the lack of masters

---

50. Nahum M. Sarna, "Exodus, Book of," ABD, vol. II, 697.

51. The "Israelite House," common to the Judean Highlands in Iron Age I (1200-1000 BCE) was designed to suggest an egalitarian family structure; not in the sense of authority, but in the sense of common quarters for each family member. See Shlomo

in Canaan creates little basis for an egalitarian motive to move to the Highlands.
3. There is no evidence that the lowland Canaanites revered Yahweh.
4. There is no archaeological or recorded evidence of a revolt in Canaan; and the revolt would have had to be extensive to involve enough numbers to explain the large population increase by the end of Iron Age I. Even though Egypt's power was waning, they were still the dominant presence in Canaan, and one would expect some Egyptian reaction to a revolt and records of an extensive unrest there.

Archeological evidence, in combination with an understanding of the sociology of the area, seriously challenges this attempt to solve the mystery.[52]

That brings us to:

The Ruralization Hypothesis

The Pastoral Nomad and Peasant Revolt Hypotheses are established names for those theories and represent the scholar's work. The following theory is called the Ruralization Hypothesis for lack of a better term, but does not represent a specific scholar's work.

Throughout the Eastern Mediterranean—from Greece to Crete and from other regional islands to the Hittite Empire in modern Turkey—there was a general economic, cultural and political collapse at the end of the Late Bronze Age and the beginning of Iron Age I. It is not clear what caused this collapse. Some believe there was an extensive drought for several years that resulted in famine.

Homer's *Iliad* is an epic thought to illustrate the collapse of the Hittite Empire that controlled Troy. The Greek Mycenaeans, victorious at

---

Bunimovitza and Avraham Faust, "Ideology in Stone," in *Biblical Archeology Review*, Vol. 28, No 4, July/August, 2002, 39.

52. See Sarna, "Exodus, Book of," ABD, vol. II, 697, for a brief discussion of the Alt, Mendenhall, Gottwald theories.

Troy, collapsed shortly thereafter, suffering extensive economic, political, and cultural degradation. The extent of the degradation is best illustrated by the loss of their written language—Linear B.

One result was the migration of these so called "Sea Peoples" to the shores of the Near East, from west of Egypt to the Lebanon. The reaction in the Near East, and specifically Canaan, to this extensive invasion was a migration out of the cities to small farms.

Cities were abandoned, and people moved to rural areas. Note, for example, the archaeological reference on the first page of this chapter to the fact that, in the Late Bronze Age, the smaller number of villages in the Judean Highlands had larger populations than the substantially larger number of villages in Iron Age I (again, see Appendix III).

This theory suggests that many of these Canaanites went to the relatively empty Judean Highlands, where they settled and acquired a new identity as Israelites. Evidence for this migration of Canaanites includes the following:

a. Other than the biblical account, which cannot be supported, no other theory satisfactorily accounts for the large population increase.

b. The four-room courtyard house plan was common to both the Judean Highlands and the Canaanite Lowlands.

c. Pottery was the same in the Judean Highlands and the Canaanite Lowlands.

d. Terrace farming, which Gottwald contended was introduced by the new inhabitants of the Highlands is now known to have resulted from an earlier known technology.[53]

e. Religious practices were common among the early Israelites and the Canaanites (e.g., both used El as a name for God, both worshiped Baal and Asherah during this period,[54] small female idols are found in both Israelite and Canaanite villages, and the Psalms are filled with Canaanite religious references).

---

53. Lemke "Israel, History of," ABD vol. 3, 538, for b., c., and d. above, the terracing "techniques…already existed at an earlier date."

54. Mark S. Smith, *The Early History of God*, 2nd ed. (Grand Rapids: Eerdmans: 2002), 7 for both d. and e. above.

"The current consensus of archaeologists is that the new settlements in the central highlands in the Iron Age, which are usually taken to be Israelite or Proto-Israelite, did not result from invasion or immigration, but that the material culture was essentially Canaanite."[55]

Both the Peasant Revolt and Ruralization Hypotheses postulate that the majority of the people that became Israelites came from Canaan, i.e., it was an internal migration.

Credible evidence currently available indicates that the biblical stories of the exodus, the wandering in the wilderness, and the conquest as related in the Torah are not historically accurate. Instead, the burden of that evidence supports the Ruralization Hypothesis.

Nevertheless, there may be echoes of history in the *Torah*/Pentateuch depiction. The oral traditions of the Patriarchs and Moses are so rich and varied that it is hard to believe they were created without some connection with the past.

While it is certainly possible that some of the people who became Israelites in the Judean Highlands were nomads from the eastern desert (modern day Saudi Arabia), and some were from a group of Hebrew nomads in the Egyptian Delta (no doubt in much smaller numbers than suggested in the book of Exodus), it seems likely that most of the future Israelites moved into that almost empty land from Canaan. But, though we feel confident the vast majority of these people came from Canaan, many mysteries remain about their identity.

It is possible that many of these "Canaanites" were Hebrews living in Canaan. If so, these Hebrews experienced their own exodus, fleeing from the Egyptian domination in Canaan and the ever present threat of being impressed into the labor force as described in the Armana letters.[56] Based on these same letters telling of slaves being sent to Egypt from Canaan, we can infer that if there were Hebrews that came to the Highlands from Egypt they may have been recently impressed from Canaan. It seems reasonable to speculate that any Hebrew nomads from Egypt who migrated

---

55. John J. Collins, "The Development of the Exodus Tradition." *Studies in Theology and Religion*, vol. 3, 1999.

56. An exchange of letters from and to the governors of small kingdoms in Canaan and Pharaoh, dated in the 14th century BCE.

to the Highlands would have invited their fellow Hebrews living in Canaan to join them—and that other Canaanites may have followed.

All Canaanites would have been attracted to the freedom from Egyptian tyranny that migration to the Highlands promised. They also may have been fleeing from the Sea Peoples that were causing such havoc in the Near East at that time. In addition to these inducements, any Hebrews among them may have wanted to escape any discrimination they may have experienced as a minority in Canaan.

This speculation hinges on the belief that there are some echoes of history, however tenuous, in the extensive oral traditions about the Patriarchs and their settling in Canaan. To reject this belief is to accept that these stories were the exclusive products of authors' imaginations several centuries later. If there are some echoes of history in those stories, there would have been Hebrews in Canaan in the Late Bronze Period. If a large part of the people that became the Israelites in the Highlands were Hebrews from Canaan, it would help explain the animosity ultimately expressed toward Canaan—perhaps stemming from long-standing grievances that often occur between majority and minority populations.

Even more speculatively, the "Aaron" and "Miriam" figures (and other "Israelites" in the wilderness) may represent resettled Canaanites who were not Hebrews. There is no textual support for this theory, but it would help explain the tensions in the text between Moses, on the one hand, and Aaron and Miriam, on the other. It would also help to explain the Israelites' repeated apostasy in the wilderness story after having allegedly witnessed incredible miracles performed by their God. This apostasy may represent the problems the Canaanites had in abandoning their gods and accepting the religion of Yahweh. The Golden Calf incident in the wilderness (Exodus 32), with the "Aaron" figure as a passive participant, may be a good example. The problems accepting an exclusive relationship with Yahweh persisted for 600 years, if we are to believe the reports of repeated instances of various forms of idolatry in 1 and 2 Kings throughout both Israel and Judah.

The different stories of the groups—possibly Canaanites, Hebrews from Egypt (and possibly Canaan), and Nomads from the desert—may have been skillfully woven together by the biblical authors and redacted during the 7th and 6th centuries BCE, thus creating the story we read today about the exodus, wandering, and settlement.

According to another theory, there were no Israelites at all until the settlement in the Judean Highlands. As previously noted, Jethro may represent a priest of Yahweh who indoctrinated the Moses figure. That may be the origin of Yahweh in the Judean Highlands brought there with Alt's desert nomads. The desert nomads and the Canaanites may have come together and become the Israelites. The Canaanites, wishing to distance themselves from other Canaanites, transferred their loyalty (although with great difficulty) from Baal and other Canaanite gods to Yahweh. This is another possible explanation of the repeated apostasy experienced during the story of the Wandering in the Wilderness.

Those who support this theory hold that the stories of the Patriarchs were fictions that were written later to create the myth of selection by Yahweh and to fabricate a glorious past. Support for this theory includes the fact that there is no extra-biblical evidence for Israel at all until the late 13th century BCE with the discovery of the Merneptah stele.

Credible opposition to this minimalist theory exists. While there is no known mention by the Egyptians of "Israel" until the late 13th century, remember that the Egyptians referred to all peoples from Canaan as "Asians." More importantly, there is a wealth of biblical material strongly suggesting a rich oral tradition predating the settlement in the Highlands, including some material less than flattering to the Patriarchs and the Israelites, and therefore more credible.[57] In addition, there is scholarly consensus that five biblical passages include archaic language and poetic structure common to an early period. In any event, these passages must be from a time well before the 7th century BCE writing or redacting of much of the biblical writings.

Conclusion

This is what we may tentatively conclude based on the evidence available to us today: The biblical stories of the Exodus, wandering in the wilderness, and the conquest of the Promised Land are not historically accurate. Nonetheless, they tell a compelling story of the escape of a people from domination to a place of freedom and greater safety. The majority of people that occupied the Judean Highlands in Iron Age I came from Canaan and not from Egypt or the desert.

---

57. E.g., Genesis 12.13; Exodus 17.2–4 and 32; Judges 2.11–13 and 19.22–27.

We cannot be certain, however, who they were. If the current lack of convincing evidence for Hebrews in Egypt and Canaan persists, we may be forced to take seriously a theory similar to the Single Exodus Model as outlined here.

The Single Exodus Model

While the biblical exodus from Egypt is a Single Exodus Model, it is untenable. However, there is a Single Exodus Model that is plausible. This Single Exodus Model postulates an exodus from Canaan, not Egypt, with Canaanites, not Hebrews, fleeing Egyptian domination. This model assumes there were no Hebrews/Israelites until Canaanites migrated to the Highlands to escape the domination they suffered from Egypt. They may have been joined there by some nomads from the dessert, who came to the Highlands for a more settled and easier life, not to escape Egyptian domination. They joined forces and forged a new identity as Israelites in time to be immortalized on the Merneptah Stele. The worship of Yahweh may have been brought to the Highlands by the nomads (represented in the Bible by Jethro/Hoban/Reuel).[58] The worship of Yahweh was accepted by this population as part of the process of distancing themselves from their former identity. Biblical hints of this origin of Yahweh worship can be found in,

- Exodus 2.15b, "He [Moses] settled in the land of Midian (a desert)."
- Exodus 18.5, "Jethro, Moses' father-in-law came into the wilderness…"
- Exodus 18.9, "Jethro rejoiced for all the good that the Lord [Yahweh!] had done to Israel…"—Exodus 18.11, "Now I [Jethro] know that the Lord [Yahweh] is greater than all gods…"

Jethro's enthusiastic embracing of Yahweh in the wilderness may very well be religious propaganda about the "born again" experience of

---

58. Mark S. Smith, *The Early History of God*, 2nd ed. (Grand Rapids: Wm. B. Eerdsman Publishing Co.: 2002), 32, "Perhaps due to trade with Edom/Midian, Yahweh entered secondarily into the Israelite highland religion." In footnote 82, p. 47, Smith writes, "Yahweh, who after all is said to derive from Midian/Teiman/Paran…"

the priest of another god. But it might also be the echo of an old oral tradition that Yahweh had been Jethro's god all along.

Many of the resettled Canaanites were resistant to accepting the religion of Yahweh, resulting in the apostasies, conflicts, and persistence of Canaanite worship patterns, e.g.,

- the incident of the making of the "Golden Calf" in the wilderness,
- the "high places,"
- the "sacred poles" (known as Asherahs although probably not identified with the Canaanite goddess of the same name).
- the worship of the Canaanite goddess Asherah and god Baal.[59]
- the 8th century BCE small female figures found in all villages that are similar to previously found Canaanite god figures except they do not have divine insignia (Frymer-Kensky suggests that these figures do not represent divinity).[60]

These religious activities, reported in the Bible and, for the most part, confirmed by archaeologists, were suppressed during reigns of reformist kings in the 8th and 7th centuries BCE (e.g., Hezekiah and Josiah), but they were never extinguished and they persisted for 600 years from the exodus (c 1200 BCE) until the exile, beginning in 597 BCE, and the final destruction of Jerusalem in 586 BCE.

In this Single Exodus Model, the patriarchal history in Genesis, as well as the stories of the exodus, wandering in the wilderness, and the conquest become fictions designed to create a glorified history and a justification for their possession of the land.

This Single Exodus Model is difficult to accept because it obliterates traditions sacred to Jews and honored by Christians including the exodus from Egypt tradition and all the traditions of the patriarchs. But, it will have to stand as a possibility until there is persuasive extra-biblical evidence for a Hebrew presence in Late Bronze Age Canaan.

---

59. Ibid., 7.

60. Tikva Frymer-Kensky, *In the Wake of the Goddesses* (New York: Fawcet Columbine: 1992).

If such evidence supporting the presence of Hebrews in Canaan does become available; or—if it is clearly established that the traditional stories are so rich that they must include echoes of history, however vague, and that a writer many hundreds of years later could not have created these complex and conflicting stories out of whole cloth—then we might come to accept something similar to this Double Exodus Model.

The Double Exodus Model

This model assumes that Hebrews (and, perhaps, others) from Canaan escaped Egyptian domination by fleeing to the Highlands, joining a small cadre of fellow Hebrews who had fled from Egypt. Perhaps those from Egypt had invited their kinsmen from Canaan to join them. Thus, there were two exodus events, a small one from Egypt and a large one from Canaan. In the stories told over campfires and at feasts, the "Moses" figure represented the nomads from Egypt. Although he represented a small minority group, the Moses story was by far the most dramatic, and it became the dominant framework around which the exodus story was finally compiled.

The stories of each group were combined, changed, integrated, embellished, augmented, and expanded to glorify the accomplishments of their hero-leaders Moses, Joshua, and others, Israelite and non-Israelite alike. While changing all the hero-leaders into Israelites from Egypt, the authors skillfully retained elements of the difficulty these non-Israelites had in accepting the religion of Yahweh and in the friction that must have existed among the groups. This Two Exodus Model retains the historical tradition of the patriarchs, which verifies the presence of Hebrews in Canaan, which makes it likely that Hebrews relocated from Canaan to Egypt to avoid the effects of drought on their livestock, and which makes the story of a Moses and some aspects of a later, relatively small, exodus from Egypt possible.

While almost all of us would be more comfortable with this model than the One Exodus Model offered above, we must wait for more evidence of the presence of Hebrews in Canaan to confidently embrace something like the Double Exodus Model.

Of course, there are many other possibilities and variations to these Single and Double Exodus Models. "In general, it is very difficult to garner more than a broad picture of Israel prior to the eight century, and at times the thesies offered [including mine above] seem conjectural."[61]

After all this analysis, we are still left with mysteries about the nature of the people who migrated to the Judean Highlands in Iron Age I.

---

61. Smith., xxii.

Appendix III

Survey of Sites by Region and Period Appearing on Settlement Maps[62]

	Late Bronze	Iron I	Iron II [63]
Judah	0	18	68
Benjamin	0	52	180
Ephraim	4	102	89
Manasseh	32	147	220
Gilead	19	77	53
Jordan Valley	20	40	41
Hesbon (in Ammon)	6	32	61
Moab[64]	0	170	98
Wadi el-Hasa (in Edom)	7	40	42
Total	88	678	852

While there are almost eight times as many Iron Age I sites as Late Bronze Age sites, the Iron Age I sites were smaller. That is why the estimated population increased by only three times from Late Bronze to Iron Age I (from about 50,000 to about 150,000).

---

62. Stager, Table 3.2, 135.

63. c. 1000—600 BCE.

64. In the absence of Mycenaean or Cypriot imported pottery and lack of local pottery with exclusively Late Bronze II characteristics, all of the Late Bronze sites in the Kerak Plateau Survey have been reassigned to the Iron Age I period.

Appendix IV

Conflicts in the Deuteronomistic History on the Conquest

The Deuteronomistic History (DtrH) includes the books of Deuteronomy, Joshua, Judges, 1 and 2 Samuel, and 1 and 2 Kings. These books are clearly connected linguistically and theologically.[65] The Deuteronomist (D) was probably a school of several authors over time with a common religious cause. The book of Deuteronomy may have been originally written either during the reign of Hezekiah (727-698 BCE), who attempted a religious reform in Judah; or Josiah's reign (639-609 BCE) when it may have been discovered in the Temple, according to 2 Kings 22.8. According to 2 Kings, the reforms mandated therein were vigorously executed by Josiah. While there is little scholarly consensus on the content of the subsequent redactions (editings) of the DtrH, it seems probable that there were redactions and additional writings of D during Josiah's reign and later during (and possibly after) the exile (586- 538 BCE). In the DtrH we find the following:

Joshua 11: "King Jabin…sent to…the king…[of] the Jebusites [people of Jerusalem]…They came out with all their troops, a great army… So, Joshua came suddenly upon them with all his fighting force…and fell upon them…They struck them down, until they had left no one remaining… all the towns of those kings, and all their kings, Joshua took, and struck with the edge of the sword, utterly destroying them, as Moses, the servant of the Lord had commanded."

Joshua 15.63: "But the people of Judah could not drive out the Jebusites, the inhabitants of Jerusalem; so the Jebusites live with the people of Judah in Jerusalem to this day."

Judges 1.8: "Then the people of Judah fought against Jerusalem and took it. They put it to the sword and set the city on fire."

Judges 1.21: "But the Benjaminites did not drive out the Jebusites who lived in Jerusalem; so the Jebusites have lived in Jerusalem among the Benjaminites to this day."

---

65. Finkelstein and Silberman, 13.

2 Samuel 5.6-7: "The king [David] and his men marched to Jerusalem against the Jebusites…David took the stronghold of Zion, which is now the city of David."

The 2 Samuel 5 passage is silent on the fate of the inhabitants, which suggests the author did not have David put the inhabitants to the sword as did Joshua and the people of Judah.

Thus, we have,

- Joshua,
- the people of Judah, and
- David

credited with the taking of Jerusalem.
And,

- Joshua and the people of Judah killing all the inhabitants, and
- The Benjamites, and, again, the people of Judah, and David apparently living with the inhabitants.

How are we to understand this conflicting attribution and result, all from the same author or author's school? Since we believe that the D authors were intelligent and skillful writers, we must assume they were entirely aware of the conflicts in their writings. I believe they simply reproduced a variety of old oral traditions important to segments of their population. Many scholars believe the earliest version of DtrH told the unified conquest story in Joshua 1-15, including the Joshua 11 and Judges 1.8 versions of the conquest and the killing of all the inhabitants of Jerusalem, along with its king. The Joshua 15.63 and Samuel 5.6-7 versions of the story might have come later based on the desire to augment the stature of David and acknowledge that the Jebusites were not exterminated in the occupying of Jerusalem. In fact, Jerusalem under the Jebusites was old and "well-established…[and] David easily could have drawn on its established bureaucracies in running the city."[66]

It is also interesting to carefully read the "David" and the tribe of

---

66. David M. Howard, Jr., "David" ABD, vol. 2, 44.

"Benjamin" passages about the conquest of Jerusalem. David is clearly glorified by his capture of Jerusalem. On the other hand, the author of the "Benjamin" passage in Judges 1.21 seems critical of the Benjaminites' inability to follow the lead of Joshua in killing all the inhabitants, although the result seems to be the same as David's.

A possible explanation of this withholding of praise for the Benjaminites is a reaction to the episode in Judges 19 and 20 telling the shameful story of the rape of the Levite's concubine by the Benjaminites and the righteous retaliation of the other tribes to it.

Sources and Additional Reading

Boling, Robert G., "Joshua, Book of," *The Anchor Bible Dictionary* (ABD). Volume 3, David Noel Freedman, et. al., eds. (New York: Doubleday: 1992).

Bunimovitza, Shlomo and Faust, Avraham, "Ideology in Stone," in Biblical Archeology Review. Vol. 28, No 4.

Calloway, Joseph A., "Ái," in ABD. Volume 1.

Collins, John J., "The Development of the Exodus Tradition." in *Studies in Theology and Religion*, vol. 3, an Willem Van Henten (The Netherlands School for Advanced Studies in Theology and Religion: 1999).

Cross, Frank Moore, *Cannanite Myth and Hebrew Epic* (Cambridge, MA: Harvard University Press: 1973).

Dever, William G., "Is There Any Archaeological Evidence for the Exodus?" in *Exodus: the Egyptian Evidence*. Frerichs, Ernest and Lesko, Leonard, Editors (Winona Lake, IN: Eisenbrauns, Inc.: 1997).

Finkelstein, Israel and Silberman, Neil Asher, *The Bible Unearthed* (New York: The Free Press: 2001).

Finkelstein, Israel, "Pots and People Revisited: Ethnic Boundaries in the Iron Age I" in *The Archeology of Israel: Constructing the Past, Interpreting the Present*. Silberman, Neil A. and Small, David, eds. (Sheffield: Sheffield Academic Press: 1997).

Frymer-Kensky, Tikva, *In the Wake of the Goddesses* (New York: Fawcet Columbine: 1992).

Gillman, Florence Morgan, "Moses" in ABD, Volume 4.

Goelet, Ogden, "Moses' Egyptian Name," *Bible Review*, Vol. XIX, no 3, June, 2003.

Hendel, Ronald S., "Exodus: A Book of Memories," Bible Review, Vol. XVIII, no 4, August, 2002.

Kitchen, K. A., "The Exodus," in ABD, Volume 2.

Holloway, Steven W., "Book of Kings," in ABD, Volume 4.

Howard, David M., "David," in ABD, Volume 2,

Lemke, Niels Peter, "Israel, History of," in ABD, Volume 3.

Levenson, Jon D., *Sinai and Zion* (New York: HarperSanFrancisco: 1985).

Mazar, Amihai, *Archaeology of the Land of the Bible—10,000—586 BCE* (New York: Doubleday: 1992).

Mercer, Samuel A. B., *The Tel-Armana Tablets, Vols. I and II* (Toronto: The Macmillan Company of Canada Limited: 1939).

Miller, Maxwell J. and Hayes, John H., *A History of Ancient Israel and Judah* (Philadelphia: The Westminster Press: 1986).

Netzer, Ehud, "Jerico," in ABD, Vol. 3.

Redford, Donald B., "Observations on the Sojourn of the Bene-Israel" in *Exodus: The Egyptian Evidence*. Ernest Frerichs and Leonard Lesko, Editors (Winona Lake, IN: Eisenbrauns, Inc.: 1992).

Redford, Donald B., *Egypt, Cannan, and Israel in Ancient Times* (Princeton, NJ: Princeton University Press: 1992).

Sarna, Nahum M., " Israel in Egypt" in *Ancient Israel*, Hershel Shanks, Editor (Washington: Biblical Archaeological Society: 1999).

Sarna, Nahum M., "Book of Exodus," in ABD, Volume 2.

Smith, Mark S., *The Early History of God*, 2nd edition (Grand Rapids: Eerdsmanns: 2002).

Stager, Lawrence E., in "Forging an Identity: The Emergence of Ancient Israel," in *Oxford History of the Biblical World*, Michael Coogan, Editor (New York: Oxford University Press: 1998).

Yurco, Frank J., "Merenptah's Canaanite Campaign and Israel's Origins" in *Exodus: The Egyptian Evidence*. Ernest Frerichs and Leonard Lesko, Editors (Winona Lake, IN: Eisenbrauns, Inc.: 1992).

Chapter 5

The Deuteronomist vs. Ahab

In this chapter we discuss some undisputed history (i.e., von Ranke's "what actually happened") in the Bible: the reign of King Ahab of the Northern Kingdom, Israel, from the early 870s to the mid 850s BCE (scholars disagree on the exact dates). Ahab is a real figure in history, and there is significant evidence that many of the political events written about in I Kings, 16.29—22.40 actually occurred.

A school of authors called the Deuteronomist (D) wrote the biblical books of Deuteronomy, Joshua, Judges, 1 and 2 Samuel, and 1 and 2 Kings. These books are referred to as the Deuteronomistic History (DtrH). A draft of the first of these books, Deuteronomy, may have been written c 621 BCE.[1] The D school probably originated in Israel and moved to The Southern Kingdom, Judah, after the conquest of Israel by the Assyrians, completed in 721 BCE.

"The Deuteronomistic and prophetic traditions single [Ahab] out as one of the worst kings of the Northern Kingdom [Israel]."[2] Ahab and his wife, Jezebel, are depicted as the epitome of evil, and their reputation has reflected this portrayal for over 2,500 years.

Is this depiction of Ahab fair and accurate, or is it slanted based on theological concerns? This chapter may cause you to change your mind about Ahab and reinstate the reputation of a much maligned king.

D seems to be conflicted about the most appropriate style of government in Israel. On the one hand, he is not pleased at the behavior of the people of Israel during the time of the Judges. In Judges 21.25 he writes,

---

1. Steven W. Holloway, "Kings, Book of 1-2" in *The Anchor Bible Dictionary* (ABD), David Noel Freedman, et. al., eds. (New York: Doubleday: 1992), Vol. 4, 71. Hollaway states that the belief that the book of Deuteronomy is related to the "book of the law" discovered in the Temple as per 2 Kings is at least as old as an observation by Origin (c 186-254 CE).
2. Wilfried Thiel, "Ahab," in ABD, Vol. 1, 100.

"In those days there was no king in Israel; all the people did what was right in their own eyes."

A commentator considers this quote as a "A final verdict on the events of chs 19-21. There is no individual (except the concubine) whose conduct is not abominably immoral."[3]

This seems to be an endorsement of human kingship. But, in fact, D preserves traditions that were opposed to human kingship. Leaving aside the United Kingdom's Saul (who D disapproves of), David (who D approves of), and Solomon (about whom D is equivocal), D approves of 8 kings of the Southern Kingdom of Judah.[4]

However, he disapproves of 11 kings of Judah.[5]

But there is only the smallest mixed bag in the Northern Kingdom, Israel. In 1 and 2 Kings, D disapproves of 18 kings of Israel, while passing no judgment on one.[6]

In spite of his disapproval of many of the kings of Judah, D glorified Judah over Israel and wrote that the cause of Israel's destruction was the lack of ritual and religious purity in Israel. Worshiping exclusively at the temple in Jerusalem, and the worship of *YHWH* exclusively, had became obsessions in Judah under kings Hezekiah (c 727-698) and Josiah (c 639-609 BCE). "The fundamental and ultimately fatal illegitimacy of the Northern Kingdom is due to the 'sin of Jeroboam,' that is, a national cult neither purely

---

3. In *The Oxford Annotated Bible: New Revised Standard Version*, Bruce M. Metzger and Roland E. Murphy, eds. (New York: Oxford University Press: 1991). Note on p. 331.

4. In 1 Kings: Asa, 15.11; Jehoshaphat, 22.43; and in 2 Kings: Jehoash, 12.2; Amaziah, 14.3; Azariah, 15.3; Jotham, 15.34; Hezekiah, 18.3; Josiah, 22.2.

5. In 1 Kings: Rehoboam, 14.22; Abijam, 15.3; and in 2 Kings: Jehoram, 8.18; Ahaziah, 8.27; Ahaz, 16.2; Manasseh, 21.2; Amon, 21.20; Jehoahaz, 23.32; Jehoiakim, 23.37; Jehoiachin, 24.9; Zedekiah, 24.19. D had to also criticize Judah, however moderately, because he had to construct a theological reason for Judah's later fall to the Babylonians and the resulting exile. See footnote 12 on Manasseh.

6. D disapproves of the following, 1 Kings: Jeroboam I, 13.33; Nadab, 15.26; Baasha, 15.34; Elah, 16.13; Zimri, 16.19; Omri, 16.25; Ahab, 16.30; Ahaziah, 22.52. In 2 Kings: Jehoram, 3.2; Jehu, 10.31; Jehoahaz, 13.2; Jehoash, 13.11; Jeroboam II, 14.24; Zechariah, 15.9; Menahem, 15.18; Pekahiah, 15.24; Pekah, 15.28; Hoshea, 17.2. He passes no judgment on Shallum, 2 Kings 15. 13-15.

Yahwistic (by the standards of DtrH) nor centralized in Jerusalem…the ecumenical spirit [of Ahab] is utterly condemned."[7]

Beginning in Chapter 16 verse 30, of 1 Kings, D tells us that,

> "Ahab son of Omri did evil in the sight of the Lord more than all who were before him… he took as his wife Jezebel daughter of King Ethbaal of the Sidonians, and went and served Baal, and worshiped him. He erected an altar for Baal in the house of Baal, which he built in Samaria. Ahab also made a sacred pole. Ahab did more to provoke the anger of the Lord, the God of Israel, than had all the kings of Israel who were before him. In his days, Hiel of Bethel built Jericho; he laid its foundations at the cost of Abiram, his firstborn, and set up its gates at the cost of his youngest son Segub, according to the word of the Lord, which he spoke by Joshua son of Nun."[8]

It is hard to imagine stronger criticism than being more evil, "than all who were before him," and to have done," more to provoke the anger of the Lord, the God of Israel, than all the kings of Israel who were before him." To support this criticism, in 1 Kings 9.7, D has Yahweh warn Solomon approximately 200 years before Ahab's reign: "If you turn aside from following me, you or your children, and do not keep my commandments and my statutes that I have set before you, but go and serve other gods, and worship them, then I will cut Israel off from the land that I have given them; and the house that I have consecrated for my name I will cast out of my sight; and Israel will become a proverb and a taunt among all peoples."

This was ostensibly a warning to Solomon, foretelling the split of

---

7. Holloway, "Kings," ABD, Vol. 4, 77. Jeroboam was instrumental in splitting Israel from Judah and was the first king of the Northern Kingdom (see 1 Kings 12). It is difficult to see how he could have accepted that worship should be exclusively in the Temple in Jerusalem, in the rival Southern Kingdom Judah, to the exclusion of any other location.

8. In Joshua 6.26, D has Joshua say, "Cursed before the Lord be anyone who tries to build this city—this Jericho! At the cost of his firstborn he shall lay the foundation, and at the cost of his youngest he shall set up the gates." As was the quote from Kings 16. 30f, Joshua 6.26 was written long after both Joshua's and Ahab's time; D may have inserted this passage in Joshua to support his case against Ahab.

the unified monarchy as the punishment for his erection of altars to other gods and promoting other idolatrous acts. However, it was written many years after the reign of Ahab and probably also targeted Ahab and the other kings of Israel who were also criticized by D.

Also, these two quotations from 1 Kings 9 and 1 Kings 16 were written well after Israel's fall: they are among the many after-the-fact prophecies in the Bible.

To summarize D's accusations, Ahab's sins were:

1. He married a Sidonian (a Phoenician, a Canaanite).
2. He erected an altar for Baal and worshiped him.
3. He made a sacred pole.
4. Ahab may have tolerated sacrifice of children to gain God's approval for the building of Jericho.

In perspective, some of these "sins" may actually be commendable (depending on your point of view), others may not have happened, and others were somewhat understandable. Let us analyze each accusation.

He married a Sidonian (i.e., a Canaanite).

"Ahab was the exponent of a political program introduced by his father, Omri, shaped mainly to counter the threat posed by the expanding power of the neighboring Aramean kingdom of Damascus…one may assume a constant state of tension between Aram-Damascus and Israel."[9] It was important for Ahab to stabilize his relationships with the other countries on his borders. He successfully made peace with Judah, and, "probably already as crown prince, married the Phoenician [i.e., Sidonian and Canaanite] princess Jezebel, daughter of Ethbaal, King of the Sidonians,"[10] to stabilize his border with Phoenicia. In addition, the

---

9. Thiel, "Ahab," ABD, 101.

10. Ibid. 101. Thiel also reports that, according to Josephus in Jewish Antiquities, Jezebel was the daughter of Ittobaal, king of Tyre and Sidon, the principal cities of Phoenicia (Sidonia). Ittobaal and Ethbaal were probably the same person.

marriage to Jezebel undoubtedly pleased his large Canaanite population. This marriage seems part of a successful foreign and domestic policy.

It is interesting to note that D thought Solomon was a great king in spite of the fact that he married foreign women for the same purpose. For example,

> "Solomon made a marriage alliance with Pharaoh king of Egypt; he took Pharaoh's daughter and brought her into the city of David (I Kings 3).
>
> Among his wives were seven hundred princesses." (1 Kings 11)

He erected an altar for Baal and worshiped him.

This may very well be a half-truth. There were fewer non-Israelites in Judah, so uniform purity of religious observance was more attainable there. But the kingdom of Israel had large Canaanite and Aramean populations, and the kings of Israel allowed those peoples to worship their own gods. Ahab almost certainly erected an altar to Baal so that Jezebel, her court, and his Canaanite population would be able to worship their principal god. He may even have participated in its opening ceremony. This was interpreted as idolatrous by the religious powers in Judah, including D, who attacked this alleged idolatry in their brother country. Today, most of us would praise Ahab for his religious tolerance and frown on Judah for their rigidity and lack of tolerance. Tolerant or not, Ahab clearly engaged in good domestic politics to "strike a balance between the Israelite population and traditional Canaanite segments of his population,"[11] keep his country together, and avoid internal strife.[12]

---

11. Ibid. 101. "Baal was identical to the Phoenician god Melkant whom Jezebel knew from her homeland."

12. Manasseh, king of Judah, was, like Ahab, tolerant of the traditional worship opposed by his father King Hezekiah and the D school. He is roundly criticized in 2 Kings 21.2f, "He did what was evil in the sight of the Lord…he rebuilt the high places that his father Hezekiah had destroyed; he erected altars for Baal, made a sacred pole, as King Ahab of Israel had done, worshiped all the host of heaven, and served them…. [he carved an] image of Asherah." D then blames the destruction of Judah and Jerusalem on these activities of Manasseh.

In another noteworthy parallel between the maligned Ahab and the celebrated Solomon, both Ahab and Solomon erected one or more altars for other gods.

"For when Solomon was old, his wives turned away his heart after other gods; and his heart was not true to the Lord his God…[he] followed Astarte the goddess of the Sidonians, and Milcom the abomination of the Ammonites…[he] built a high place for Chemosh the abomination of Moab, and for Molech the abomination of the Ammonites on the mountain east of Jerusalem. He did the same for all his foreign wives, who offered incense and sacrificed to their gods." (1 Kings 11.4f)

D reports God's anger at this apostasy as 1 Kings 11 continues,

"Then the Lord was angry with Solomon, because his heart had turned away from the Lord…'since…you have not kept my covenant and my statutes…I will surely tear the kingdom from you and give it to your servant. Yet for the sake of your father David I will not do it in your lifetime; I will tear it out of the hand of your son. I will not, however, tear away the entire kingdom; I will give one tribe to your son, for the sake of my servant David, and for the sake of Jerusalem, which I have chosen.'"

The "servant" here is Jeroboam I, the first king of Israel when it broke away from the Southern Kingdom under King Rehoboam, the son of Solomon. This is another example of accurate predictions written long after the predicted events occurred.

The main point is that Solomon had many more foreign wives than Ahab did and also erected altars to foreign gods. Yet D judges Ahab as being more evil, "than all were before him," while Solomon, although criticized for similar behavior by God, is not severely judged by D.

One reason for the softer treatment of Solomon was Judah's (and D's) obsession about the Davidic line. Solomon was a son of David; David was not an ancestor of Ahab.

Regarding the accusation that Ahab worshipped Baal, Ahab was, "hardly a Baal worshipper;...the names of his sons Ahaziah and Jehoram contained the root of Yahweh's name, and these names were Ahab's way of demonstrating his attachment to the God of Israel.[13]

He made a sacred pole (an Asherah).

Like the previous "sin," the raising of Asherahs pleased a large part of his population who traditionally had raised sacred poles. These wooden poles were probably raised by both Canaanites and Israelites. Almost all scholars would agree they were objects of veneration, but there is dispute over what kind of veneration. There is little evidence available, and general disagreement among scholars, as to the exact purpose of sacred poles (Asherahs) in Israel. Some scholars believe, "Sacred poles were symbols of the Canaanite fertility goddess Asherah...mentioned about 40 times in the Hebrew Scriptures as a temptation to the Israelites."[14] The "temptation" referred to in this quotation is an alarm sounded by D, a radical monotheist, who opposed any aspect of worship or veneration not exclusively dedicated to Yahweh. While, "most scholars believe that Asherah was a goddess in monarchic Israel...it has not been [proven], given the plausibility of alternative views."[15]

"Perhaps this 'Asherah' is to be seen as a native Israelite goddess...All the evidence in both the Bible and the inscriptions indicates that 'Asherah' was associated with the cult of *YHWH* rather than any cult of Ba'al."[16] Some scholars believe that the aridity of the land made fertility gods and goddesses popular with all peoples. The story beginning in 1 Kings 18 of the three-year drought relieved by Elijah's prayer to Yahweh may be an effort to establish Yahweh as a god of fertility as well as a protector of Israel.

---

13. Thiel, "Ahab," ABD, Vol. 1, 102.

14. *The New Oxford Annotated Bible* (NOAB), Bruce Metzger and Roland Murphy, editors (New York: Oxford University Press, 1991), note to 1 Kings 14.15, 448.

15. Mark S. Smith, *The Early History of God*, 2nd ed. (Grand Rapids and Cambridge, UK: Wm. B. Eerdsmans Publishing Company, 2002), xxxii, xxxvi.

16. Tikva Frymer-Kenski, *In the Wake of the Goddesses* (New York: Fawcett Columbine, 1992), 158.

He may have tolerated the sacrifice of children in the building of Jericho.

"In his days Hiel of Bethel built Jericho; he laid its foundation at the cost of Abiram his firstborn, and set up its gates at the cost of his youngest son Segub, according to the word of the Lord, which he spoke by Joshua, son of Nun."(1 Kings 16.34)

"Cursed before the lord be anyone who tries to build this city—this Jericho! At the cost of his firstborn he shall lay the foundation, and at the cost of his youngest he shall set up its gates!" (Joshua 6. 26)

These remarkable passages were both written by D at least 150 years after Ahab's time.

Since almost all scholars believe that the story of Joshua's taking of Jericho is a myth, Joshua could not have actually voiced that curse. The most logical conclusion is that D retrojected the curse into the book of Joshua to add support for his case against Ahab.

But why a curse on Jericho? Joshua reputedly destroyed many other cities without laying a curse on anyone who would rebuild them (e.g., Lachish in Joshua 10.11, Hebron in Joshua 10.36, and Hazor in Joshua 11.11 among many others). All these cities were subsequently rebuilt without any reported adverse consequences. An increasing number of scholars argue that these passages are not about Hiel's sacrifice of two of his children to insure the project's success, but rather suggest that the premature death of Hiel's children was his penalty for rebuilding Jericho. The vagueness of the accusation supports this conclusion. If child sacrifice was the charge, you would think that D, a competent writer, would have made that explicit and graphic by writing something like,

> "...he offered up his firstborn as a burnt offering in laying its foundation, etc."

After all, in Judges 11.32, D describes a human sacrifice in those graphic terms,

> "Whoever comes out of the doors of my house to meet me, when I return victorious from the Ammonites shall be the Lord's, to be offered up by me as a burnt offering."

The one who said those words was Jephthah, an Israelite hero. Why would D have pulled his punches in describing a child sacrifice attributed, however indirectly, to Ahab?

One scholar points out the parallel between the early deaths of Hiel's two children and the early deaths of Ahab's two children (Ahaziah and Jehoram) both of whom died in accordance, "with the word of the Lord," because both Hiel and Ahab engaged in construction against the will of the Lord (in Hiel's case—Jericho; in Ahab case—a temple and altar to Baal).[17]

Thus, the evidence we have seems to indicate that it is unlikely that the deaths of Hiel's two sons was an instance of child sacrifice.

Finally, we should remember that child sacrifice had been a long-standing method of insuring success throughout the Ancient Near East, including in Israel. Human sacrifice was probably very rare at this time in Israel's history, and the practice would soon disappear altogether.

Thus, at least the first three of Ahab's alleged sins can be seen as the actions of an effective king. It is interesting to note that we have all been taught to hate Ahab and Jezebel for a reason most of us now emphatically support; i.e., religious tolerance. Also, Ahab's marriage to Jezebel can be seen as simply good politics, somewhat analogous to an American presidential candidate balancing his ticket with a careful choice of a Vice Presidential running mate.

More difficult to justify is the story in 1 Kings 21 where Ahab forcefully took a piece of land from Naboth after Naboth rejected Ahab's offer to provide him a better property, saying,

"The Lord forbid that I should give you my ancestral inheritance."

It was, "well established-legal and religious custom [that] ancestral property must remain in the family in perpetuity" (Lev. 25.10, 13-17, 23-24, 34).[18]

D wrote that Jezebel falsely accused the owner of blasphemy and had him killed. We do not know how D may have slanted the story

---

17. Charles Conroy, "Animadversiones" in *Biblica*, vol. 77, no. 2, (1996) 210-218.
18. NOAB, note to 1 Kings 21.1-4, 458, OT.

against Ahab, but, if true, the killing of the owner in order to possess the property is reprehensible. Nevertheless, Kings, Emperors, Presidents, and other heads of national and local governments have taken property from their owners for thousands of years, and our national and local governments continue that practice today, condemning property for the "national interest" or for the "development of needed community improvements."

The story in 1 Kings illustrates the conflict arising from the ancient law written in Leviticus 25, which indicates that "the Lord owns the land and gives it to the people of Israel for stewardship."[19] versus the right of kings to confiscate property.

Conclusion

D's theological bias creates propaganda which obscures the positive results obtained by Ahab.

1. His reign increased the prosperity in Israel (which was much wealthier than Judah), following the legacy of his father, King Omri, who initiated the most successful dynasty in Israel's history.[20]
2. He built many important projects. Some have been attributed to Solomon, but recent archaeological evidence may suggest that they should be attributed to Ahab, or his father Omri, as the king responsible for the projects.[21]
3. He was an important part (supplying the largest contingent of chariots) of the alliance that defeated the army of Shalmaneser III, king of Assyria, at the battle of Qarqar in 853 BCE, delaying the eventual destruction of Israel for an additional 132 years.

---

19. Ibid., note to Lev. 25, 157.
20. Israel Finkelstein and Neil Asher Silberman, *The Bible Unearthed* (New York: The Free Press: 2001), 186-195.
21. Finkelstein and Silberman, 183, 186, 187.

None of these achievements are reported in the DtrH; clearly a case of selective reporting.

Winfried Thiel concludes his essay on Ahab in *The Anchor Bible Dictionary* as follows:

> "The portrait of Ahab and his dynasty (the "House of Ahab") has been negatively distorted in the OT [Old Testament] tradition primarily because of his religious policies which were seen as a danger to the traditional worship of God in circles loyal to Yahweh. His skillful foreign policies, which provided Israel with strength, security and prosperity, which safeguarded peace and the balance of power, and which finally contributed to the (temporary) containment of Assyrian expansionism, may be inferred from the few sources that yield reliable historical data. However, his contributions in this regard were ignored in the decidedly theological perspective of the OT witnesses."[22]

I would add to this conclusion Ahab's policy of tolerating the religions of his queen and large segments of his population, a tolerance that infuriated D and other powers in Judah.

We must recall, however, that in antiquity, religious cults and imperial power were inter-related. Ahab's tolerance may have been practically and politically motivated, and not at all based on philosophical belief, as ours is today.

Ahab's antagonists, Elijah, and his successor, Elisha, were rigidly intolerant, yet we tend to honor them for the strength of their faith. Perhaps we should consider honoring Ahab for his political, military, and financial skill and success as a king—and for a policy of religious tolerance extended to his diverse population, however motivated.

As we have seen in the first four chapters, the theologians and scribes who authored the Bible contributed many positive key concepts necessary to the positive growth and advancement of Western civilization.

But here, in Chapter 5 we find that those same theologians and

---

22. Thiel, "Ahab," ABD, 103. The "few sources that yield reliable historical data" are: the monolith inscription of the Assyrian king Shalmaneser III, the inscription of King Mesha of Moab, and (of more doubtful value) the excerpts from the historical work of Menander of Ephesus quoted by Josephus.

scribes may have provided a rationalization for religious and ethnic intolerance and hatred in Western civilization. This hatred is advanced most aggressively by D, not only with respect to Ahab and the worshipers of Baal, but throughout the books for which D is responsible.

While fear, distrust, and even hatred of "the other" was common throughout the ANE (and the world) for millennia, most other cultures honored all the gods. Indeed, Israelites in more ancient times also honored and even worshiped other gods. But by the 8th and 7th centuries BCE, the reformers under Kings Hezekiah and Josiah began to rigidly worship and honor Yahweh exclusively, and abhor other gods. For example, recall that D refers, in 1 Kings 11, to, "Milcom the abomination of the Ammonites…Chemosh the abomination of Moab, and…Molech the abomination of the Ammonites."

Religious and ethnic hatred has plagued Western civilization for well over 2,000 years, resulting in millions of deaths and the disgraceful treatment of those whose religious beliefs or ethnic background did not correspond to some standard proposed by a religious or civil authority.

Joshua's extermination of the Canaanites and Elijah's killing of 450 prophets of Baal in 1 Kings 18. 40 are only two examples of D's idea of appropriate murderous action. A literal reading of the aforementioned Elijah passage could justify the killing of the leaders of different religions deemed to be competitive and threatening. We cannot help but wonder if D's influence can be traced to the killings associated with the Crusades, the Inquisition, the slaughter of the Huguenots and many others during the 16th and 17th century religious controversies. The Holocaust may have also been encouraged by D's influence in Western civilization. All of these events occurred either in the name of religion or in countries with strong religious traditions and authority. It is likely that Western civilization's responsibility for these atrocities can be traced to our ancestors' belief that the Bible's messages should be taken at face value as God's pronouncements.

We can only wonder what the result would have been if D had embraced religious and ethnic tolerance instead of religious and ethnic hatred.

Sources and Additional Reading

Conroy, Charles, "Animadversiones" in *Biblica*, vol. 77, no. 2, (1996).

Finkelstein, Israel and Silberman, Neil Asher, *The Bible Unearthed* (New York: The Free Press: 2001).

Frymer-Kenski, Tikva, *In the Wake of the Goddesses* (New York: Fawcett Columbine: 1992).

Holloway, Steven W., "Kings, Book of 1-2" in *The Anchor Bible Dictionary* (ABD) David Noel Freedman, et. al., eds. (New York: Doubleday: 1992), Vol. 4.

The Oxford Annotated Bible: New Revised Standard Version, Bruce M. Metzger and Roland E. Murphy, eds. (New York: Oxford University Press: 1991).

Thiel, Winfried, "Ahab," in ABD, Vol. 1.

Epilogue

Perhaps the best single sentence ever written to describe the interplay between history and myth is from Karen Armstrong's book, *A History of God*.[1] In discussing the developments that led to the writing of the gospels, which began some forty years after Jesus' death, she writes,

> "By that time, historical facts had been overlaid with mythical elements which expressed the meaning Jesus had acquired for his followers."

One can delete "Jesus" and substitute Moses, David, George Washington, or almost any other character who has inspired his or her followers. If we understand the way this mechanism works and the inherent human need for creating myths in order to find meaning, we will then be on our way to a better understanding of the Bible.

The Bible has contributed the seeds of many new and positive concepts to Western civilization. Among them are the following:

- God created mankind to have power and authority on earth, not to be a slave to the gods as in the Mesopotamian creation myths, (Gen. 1.26)
- God cares about mankind's treatment of others. (e.g., Gen. 9.6, Lev. 19)
- God loves his people, has compassion for them, and forgives them when they repent. (Ex. 34.6-7, Numbers 14.18, Jonah 4.2)
- God endorses freedom and a safe place to live for his people. (Exodus)

But the DtrH books of the Bible may have also justified and modeled slavery and discrimination, and religious and ethnic intolerance, all of which have contributed to the death of millions of people and the

---

1. Brought to my attention by Ron Miller, head of the Department of Religion at Lake Forest College in Lake Forest, Illinois.

disgraceful treatment of millions more. Unlike the positive contributions listed above, which may have been conceptual innovations, racial and ethnic hatred had had a long history before D came upon the scene; but the Bible's worst contribution to that history, through D, may have been the depiction of the extermination of "the other." Incidentally, it is not a coincidence that none of the major positive contributions to Western civilization originated in the writings of the DtrH.

Also at fault is the belief that all of the Bible is the word of God. That belief logically leads to the justification of slavery, discrimination, religious intolerance, and selected killing.

One can hope we can continue to develop the positive concepts we have learned from the Bible while rejecting the hatred based on religious, ethnic, and racial intolerance.

The author of the Holiness Code in Leviticus 19.18, 34 has God tell us: "You shall love your neighbor as yourself;" And, especially, "The alien…shall be to you as the citizen among you; you shall love the alien as yourself."

It is unfortunate that D either was unaware of this divine law or did not consider it when advocating the destruction of Canaanite aliens and Israelite neighbors who did not follow the religious practices advocated by Judah.

Index

Aaron, 78, 78*n*9, 104
Abbot, George, 6
Abel, 31, 40, 55, 56, 63
Abijam, 118*n*5
Abimelech, 21, 22, 23
Abiram, 119, 124
Abraham, E on, 18*n*18, 19, 22, 23, 24; J on, 16, 17, 19–21, 22–24, 29, 30, 31; P on, 37; stories about, xii, xxi
Abram, 20–21, 22, 23, 24, 32*n*43, 40. *see also* Abraham
Adam, J on, 16, 17, 31, 38–39, 52–53, 54–55, 68; meaning of, 41, 47, 47*n*19, 48–49, 62; Mesopotamian myths and, 45, 46; P on, 40, 64
Ahab, xiv, 117–29, 118*n*6, 119*n*8
Ahaziah, 118*n*5, 118*n*6, 123, 125
Akkadians, Akkadian language, 42, 42*n*9, 43–44, 57, 58, 95*n*45
Alt, Albrecht, 98, 99, 100, 105
Alter, Robert, 51, 70
Amaziah, 3*n*6, 118*n*4
Ammonites, 122, 124, 128
Amon, 118*n*5
Amorites, 78, 83
Amos, 3*n*6, 3*n*7, 29, 73
Anakim, 82
Apostles Creed, 2*n*4
Arad, king of, 30, 81, 89
Arameans, 25, 27, 27*n*30, 120, 121
Armana letters, 95, 95*n*45, 98, 103, 103*n*56
Armstrong, Karen, 131
Arpachshad, 62

Asa, 118*n*4
Asher, 83
Asherahs, xiii, 107, 123
"Asians," "Asiatics," 86, 86*n*27, 105
Assyrians, xi, xxii, 1, 4, 5, 7, 25, 27, 27*n*32, 29, 67, 89, 94, 117, 127, 127*n*22
Astruc, Jean, 11
Atrahasis myth, 43, 43*n*11, 44, 45–46, 46*n*17, 57–60, 63
Azariah, 118*n*4

Baasha, 118*n*6
Babel, Tower of, 53*n*27, 55, 66–67
Babylonians, xi, xiii, xxi, xxii, 7, 42, 67, 94, 118*n*5
Behemoth, 41
Benjamin, Benjaminites, 83, 111, 112–13
Ben Sirach, 50
brains, human, 51*n*25

Cain, 31, 40, 47*n*19, 55, 56, 63
camels, 20–21, 22, 30, 99
Campbell, Anthony F., 40
Canaan, 64, 65
Canaanites, D on, 24, 25; Egyptians and, 86, 90–93, 95, 98, 101; Israelites and, 61*n*40, 64–65, 78, 79, 80, 81, 82, 86, 89, 94, 100–101, 102–8, 120–21, 123, 128, 132
childbirth, difficulty in, 51, 54
Columbus, Christopher, 66
Conquest, of the Promised Land, xix, 25, 26, 75, 76, 79, 81–84, 90–98, 103, 105–6, 111–13
creation myth, xii, xiii–xiv, 37–74
Crusades, 128
Cyrus, xv

133

Danites, 83

David, xii, xxi, 25, 26, 29, 30, 31, 91, 112–13, 118, 122

D (Deuteronomist) authors, *vs.* Ahab, 117–29; on Conquest story, xiv, 94, 97, 111–13; dating of, 33; on David and Solomon, 29; Deuteronomistic History of, 24–26, 25*n*27, 111, 112–13, 117, 127, 131–32; Documentary Hypothesis and, 11, 12; E and, 32; God of, 17, 122; J and, 31–32, 34; on Moses, 16, 80*n*13; P and, xv, 24; on redemption, 28; vocabulary of, 18*n*17

dietary laws, 13, 13*n*9, 64, 64*n*44

Diodorus Siculus, 85

Documentary Hypothesis, 11–34

Double Exodus Model, 108–9

Early Bronze Age, 89, 90

Ecclesiasticus, book of, 50

Eden, expulsion from, 52–57, 68

Edom, king of, 81, 89

E (Elohist), D and, 26, 32, 34; dating of, 32; Documentary Hypothesis and, 11, 12, 13, 15, 18–19, 18*n*18; on Genesis, 21–22; God of, 18, 19; J and, 15, 18, 19, 22, 23–24, 28, 29, 32, 32*n*43, 33; P and, 19, 32, 33, 34; vocabulary of, 18*n*17

Egyptians, Egyptian language, Babylonians and, xxii, 78*n*10, 79, 101, 103, 104, 105, 108; Canaanites and, 86, 90–93, 95, 98, 101; on God, 67; Hykos and, 90; Israelites and, xxii, 76–80, 78*n*9, 84–88, 86*n*26, 95, 99; plagues of, 78, 78*n*10, 78*n*11, 84, 85; Sea Peoples and, 84*n*20

Elah, 118*n*6

Elijah, 3*n*6, 18*n*17, 123, 127, 128

Elisha, 127

Enuma Elish, 42, 43, 44, 45, 46, 57

Ephraim, 83

Esau, 19, 23, 29

Essay Concerning Human Understanding (Locke), 66

Ethbaal, 119, 120, 120*n*10

Etz Hayim, 95

Eve, J on, 16, 17, 31, 38, 39, 49–50, 51, 52, 53, 54–55, 68; meaning of, 41, 47, 47*n*19, 48–49; Mesopotamian myths and, 45

Exodus myth, xii, xix, xx, 25, 75–80, 84, 84*n*20, 85–88, 93, 95, 96, 98, 103–9

Ezekiel, xiv, xv

Ezra, xv, 40

Faulkner, William, 41

flood myth, xiii, xix, xx–xxi, xxi*n*7, 44*n*13, 57–66, 68

forgiveness, 6

forty, the number, xix, 17, 80–81, 97

freedom, xv, xix, xx, 50, 96, 97–98, 131

Frymer-Kensky, Tikva, 56, 107

Gadites, 81

Gershom, 77

Gilgamesh Epic, 42, 44, 46*n*17, 50, 57, 58, 63

Golden Calf, 104, 107

Gottwald, Norman K., 100–101, 102

Greeks, Greek language, 65, 71, 77

Gunkel, Hermann, 27

Ham, 64–65

Hammurapi, Code of, 60

Harris Papyrus I, 95

hatred, religious and ethnic, 127–28, 132

Hebrew Bible, Hebrew language, xv,

70–71, 72–73, 77, 87
Hebrews. *see* Israelites
Hendel, Ronald, xxii, 22, 26, 29, 82n16, 97
Hezekiah, xiv, 25, 25n26, 25n27, 94, 107, 111, 118, 118n4, 121n12, 128
H (Holiness Code), school of, 15, 34, 34n45, 132. *see also* P (Priestly Writers)
Hiel, 119, 124, 125
History of God, A (Armstrong), 131
Hittites, 78, 81, 82, 101
Hivites, 78, 82
Hobab, 77
Hoban, 106
Holocaust, 128
Homer, 101
Hosea, 18n17, 32
Hoshea, 118n6
Huguenots, slaughter of, 128

Iliad (Homer), 101
Inquisition, 128
intolerance, religious and ethnic, 127–28, 131–32
Iron Age I, camels in, 20–21, 99; Conquest story and, 90–91, 95, 99, 100, 100n51, 110; Double Exodus Model and, 109; Late Bronze Age and, 110n64; Pastoral Nomad Hypothesis and, 98, 99; Peasant Revolt Hypothesis and, 100–101; population in, 75, 95, 99, 100, 101, 102, 103, 110; Ruralization Hypothesis and, 102, 103, 105; Wandering in the Wilderness story and, 89
Isaac, 18n18, 20, 22–23, 24, 32n43, 37
Isaiah, 3n6
Israelis, 97
Israelites, agricultural problems of, 52; Arameans and, 120; Asherahs of, xiii, 123; Assyrians and, xi, xxii, 1, 4, 5, 7, 25, 27, 94, 117, 127; Babylonians and, xi, xiii, xxi, xxii, 7–8, 94, 118n5; Canaanites and, 61n40, 64–65, 78, 79, 80, 81, 82, 89, 94, 100–101, 102–8, 120–21, 123, 128, 132; Egyptians and, xxii, 76–80, 78n9, 84–88, 86n26, 95, 99; in exile, xi–xvi, 38, 68; J on, 29–30; as Jews, 6n11; Joshua on, 81–82, 83–84; at Kadesh-barnea, 29–30, 81, 88–89, 89n29; Moses on, 78n9, 79, 81, 93, 95, 104; origin of, 25, 75–115, 75n1; other gods worshiped by, 128; Passover and, 78n10; P on, xiv–xv, 13n7, 14–15, 37, 87–88; return to Jerusalem of, xv; Shem ancestor of, 65; using Akkadian language, 44; on water above the sky, 14
Ittobaal, 120n10

Jabin, 111
Jacob, 19, 23, 27, 37, 76, 85
James, 93
Japheth, 64, 65
Jebusites, 78, 82, 83, 111
Jehoahaz, 118n5, 118n6
Jehoash, 118n4, 118n6
Jehoiachin, 118n5
Jehoiakim, 118n5
Jehoram, 118n5, 118n6, 123, 125
Jehoshaphat, 118n4
Jehu, 118n6
Jephthah, 125
Jeremiah, 3n6
Jeroboam I, 118, 118n6, 119n7, 122
Jeroboam II, 1, 118n6
Jesus Christ, xix, 2n4, 14n10, 71, 72, 93, 96, 97, 131

Jethro, 77, 99, 105, 106–7
Jewish Publication Society, xxii, 70
Jezebel, 117, 119, 120–21, 120n10, 121n11, 125
John, xix, 93
Jonah, xviii, 1–7, 2n3, 2n4, 3n5, 3n6, 3n7, 3n8, 4n9, 8
Joseph, xviii–xix, xviiin4, 18n18, 19, 76, 83
Josephus, 120n10, 127n22
Joshua, conquest and, 91, 91n34, 92; D on, 26, 111, 112, 113, 119, 119n8, 124, 128; E on, 18; God speaking to, 93; in Double Exodus Model, 108; on Israelites, 81–82, 83–84; J on, 87
Josiah, 25, 31, 33, 94, 107, 111, 118, 118n4, 128
Jotham, 118n4
Judah, 83, 94
J (Yahwist), creation stories of, 12, 14, 15, 16, 17, 19–20, 22–23, 38–39, 42–56, 58, 59, 60, 62, 63, 64–65, 66, 67, 68; D and, 26, 34; dating of, 27–32; Documentary Hypothesis and, 11, 15; E and, 15, 22, 23–24, 28, 29, 32, 32n43, 33; God of, 13, 16, 17, 39, 46, 60, 69; on Moses, 87, 88; P and, 34, 39–40

Kenyon, Kathleen, 90

Laban, 19, 27
Lagash, Rulers of, 58
Late Bronze Age, Conquest story and, 91, 95; Edom in, 89n30; Exodus in, 85; Iron Age I and, 110n64; in Judean Highlands, 75; Moab, Edom, and Ammon in, 29; Pastoral Nomad Hypothesis and, 99; Peasant Revolt Hypothesis and, 100; population in, 95, 99, 102, 110; Ruralization Hypothesis and, 101–2, 104; Single Exodus Model and, 107; Wandering in the Wilderness story and, 88–90
Late Iron Age, 89n29
Levenson, Jon, 80
Leviathan, 41
Levite, 113
Locke, John, 66

Manasseh, xiv, 81, 83, 118n5, 121n12
Mark, 73
Matthew, 73
Medes, 7
Menahem, 118n6
Menander of Ephesus, 127n22
Mendenhall, George, 100–101
Merneptah, Merneptah Stele, 86, 86n26, 105, 106
Mesha, 127n22
Mesopotamian myths, xx, 41–46, 57–64, 68, 69, 131
Methuselah, 64
Middle Bronze Age, 21
Miller, Ron, 131n1
Miriam, 77, 87, 104
Mizner, Wilson, xvii
Moses, 76n2, birth story of, 77–78, 87–88; death of, 16, 62, 80n13; D on, 31–32, 80n13, 111; E on, 18, 19; in Exodus, 77n6, 99, 100, 106, 108; God speaking to, xiii, 3n8, 13, 37, 80, 93, 93n40, 97; on Israelites, 78n9, 79, 81, 93, 95, 104; Jethro and, 105, 106; J on, 63, 87, 97; name of, 77, 85, 87; oral traditions of, xxi, 103; P on, 13, 15, 16, 31–32, 37, 87–88; Rameses and, 84; on *Torah,* 40
Mycenaeans, 101–2

Naboth, 125
Nadab, 118*n*6
Nahum, xviii, 1, 7–8
Naphtali, 83
Nehemiah, 40
Nephilim, 61, 62
New Oxford Annotated Bible (NOAB), 1, 51
New Revised Standard Version of the Bible (NRSV), 55, 70
New Testament (NT), 72, 73, 93, 96
Nicene Creed, 2*n*4
Ninevites, 5
Noah, animals as food for, 54; Atrahasis compared to, 59; flood story of, xx–xxi, 44*n*13, 59–66; J on, 16, 17, 63, 97; P on, 40, 56, 57; sons of, 40, 55, 64, 65, 66, 67
Noth, Martin, 11, 91, 98, 99, 100
NRSV. *see* New Revised Standard Version of the Bible (NRSV)
Nun, 87, 119, 124

O'Brien, Mark A., 40
Old Testament (OT), xv, 72, 127
Omri, 118*n*6, 119, 120, 126
"other, the," 82, 82*n*16, 97, 128, 132

Palestinians, 97
Pandora's box, 50
parables, 5, 96
Passover, 78*n*10, 96
Pastoral Nomad Hypothesis, 98–99
Paul, 2*n*4, 73
Peasant Revolt Hypothesis, 100, 103
Pekahiah, 118*n*6
Pentateuch, xi, xvi, 11–34, 37, 72, 103
Perizzites, 78, 82
Persians, xv

Peter, 93
Pharaoh(s). *see also specific Pharaohs*, Armana letters to, 95, 95*n*45, 98, 103*n*56; D on, 31–32, 121; E on, 22; on Israelites, xxii, 76–77, 78, 78*n*9; J on, 20, 97; Joseph and, xviii*n*4; Moses and, 31–32, 87, 88, 99; P on, 31–32; on slavery, 76–77, 95
Philistines, 65, 79
Phoenicians, 120
P (Priestly Writers), 1, on Adam, 47; creation story of, 12, 14, 15, 17, 37, 42–43, 55, 60, 62–63, 64, 65, 68, 71; D and, xiv–xv, 24, 34; dating of, 26, 38; Documentary Hypothesis and, 11, 12, 14, 15, 17; E and, 32, 33; God of, 12, 13, 16, 17, 37–38, 39, 56–57, 60, 67, 69; on Israelites, xiv–xv, 13*n*7, 14–15, 37, 87–88; J and, 27, 31–32, 34, 39–40; on sin, 49
Prolegomena to the History of Ancient Israel (Wellhausen), 26
Prophets, xvi
Puah, 76–77, 85, 87

Rahab, 41, 82
Rameses, 77
Rameses II, 84, 85, 86, 95
Rameses III, 92, 95
Rameses IV, 98
Rameses VI, 92
Rashi, 51, 70
Rebekah, 23, 24, 32*n*43
Red Sea, parting of, 79–80
Rehoboam, 118*n*5, 122
Rendsburg, Gary, 78*n*10
Reubenites, 81
Reuel, 77, 106
Rofè, 15–16, 33–34

Romans, 71
Ruralization Hypothesis, 101–5

sacrifices, 62–63, 99, 120, 122, 124–25
Samuel, 18n17, 73, 112
Sarah, Sarai, 20, 21, 22, 23, 24, 32n43
Saul, 32, 118
Sea Peoples, 84n20, 102, 104
Segub, 119, 124
Septuagint, 71, 77, 79
Seth, 47n19
Shallum, 118n6
Shalmaneser III, 126, 127n22
Shem, 40, 64, 65, 66n49
Sheshonq I, 28
Shiphrah, 76–77, 85, 87
Sidonians, 119, 120–21, 122
Simeon, 83, 94
Simon, Richard, 11
Single Exodus Model, 106–8
slaves, slavery, xv, xx, 65, 69, 85, 95, 103, 131, 132
Smith, Joseph, 66n49
Solomon, xii, xxi, 25, 26, 27, 28, 29, 30, 31, 118, 119–20, 121, 122, 126
Sumerian Flood Story, 57–58, 63
Sumerian King List, 58
Sumerians, Sumerian language, 42, 42n9, 43, 49, 49n24, 58, 66
Syrians, 27

Tel-Armana Tablets, 95, 95n45, 98, 103, 103n56
Thiel, Winfried, 127
Tigay, Jeffrey, 67
tolerance, religious, 69, 125, 127
Torah, biblical stories in, 11–34, 11n1, 103; disobedience of, 97; Moses on, 40; origins of, xi, xvi, 12; P on, 15, 37; of United Synagogues of Conservative Judaism, The, 95
Transfiguration, the, 93
Tree of Life, 95
Tribes of Yahweh, The (Gottwald), 100
Tuthmose, 77
United Synagogues of Conservative Judaism, The, 95
Utnapishtim, 57

van Wolde, Ellen, 61
von Ranke, Leopold, xviii, xviii$n$2, 41, 117

Wandering in the Wilderness story, xix, 25, 31, 76, 80–81, 88–90, 97, 99, 103, 105–9
Wellhausen, Julius, 26
Westermann, Claus, 40, 42n9, 47, 49, 55–56

Yitzhaki, Shlomo, 48n22
Yurco, Frank, 88

Zechariah, 118n6
Zedekiah, 118n5
zero, 71
Zimmer, Carl, 51n25
Zimri, 118n6
Zipporah, 77